T0355589

 THE COMMON CORE STATE STANDARDS IN LITERACY SERIES

A series designed to help educators successfully
implement CCSS literacy standards in K–12 classrooms

SUSAN B. NEUMAN AND D. RAY REUTZEL, EDITORS

SERIES BOARD: Diane August, Linda Gambrell, Steve Graham, Laura Justice,
Margaret McKeown, and Timothy Shanahan

Revitalizing Read Alouds

Interactive Talk About Books with Young Children, PreK–2

Lisa Hammett Price
Barbara A. Bradley

Foreword by Sharon Walpole

TEACHERS COLLEGE PRESS

TEACHERS COLLEGE | COLUMBIA UNIVERSITY
NEW YORK AND LONDON

Published by Teachers College Press, 1234 Amsterdam Avenue, New York, NY 10027

Cover design by Laura Duffy Design. Photo from iStockphoto LP.

Figure 3.1 is reprinted from *Contemporary Educational Psychology*, *8*(3), P. David Pearson & Margaret C. Gallagher, "The Instruction of Reading Comprehension," pp. 317–344, Copyright © 1983, with permission from Elsevier.

The image in Figure 6.2 under the heading "Pictures with Captions" originally appeared in *Time for Kids: Frogs*, and is reprinted by permission of HarperCollins Publishers.

The unpublished poem featured in Figure 7.1, "Pitter Patter, Pitter Pat" by S. Hollingsworth (2015), is reprinted by permission of the author.

Library of Congress Cataloging-in-Publication Data is available at loc.gov

Names: Price, Lisa Hammett. | Bradley, Barbara A.
Title: Revitalizing read alouds : interactive talk about books with young children, preK-2
    / Lisa Hammett Price, Barbara A. Bradley.
Description: New York, NY : Teachers College Press, [2016] | Series: The common core state
    standards in literacy series | Includes bibliographical references and index.
Identifiers: LCCN 2015046219 (print) | LCCN 2016002876 (ebook)
ISBN 9780807757635 (pbk. : alk. paper) | ISBN 9780807774755
Subjects: LCSH: Oral reading. | Language arts (Early childhood)—United States. |
    Language arts (Elementary)—United States.
Classification: LCC LB1573.5 .P74 2016 (print) | LCC LB1573.5 (ebook) | DDC
372.45/2—dc23
LC record available at http://lccn.loc.gov/2015046219

ISBN 978-0-8077-5763-5 (paper)
ISBN 978-0-8077-7475-5 (ebook)

Printed on acid-free paper
Manufactured in the United States of America

23 22 21 20 19 18 17 16   8 7 6 5 4 3 2 1

Contents

Foreword

"What did you learn in school today?" asked a caregiver. "Nothing," replied a morose child. That conversation happens all over the country. And the children are not lying. What they have in common is placement in classrooms where read alouds are not central. The role of read alouds as an essential component of the early childhood curriculum, rather than as dessert, is a matter of core values. I consider knowledge-building as the most important goal of schooling. Knowledge builds strategies; knowledge fuels self-direction; knowledge fuels self-efficacy. All children can learn new things. In fact, they like to learn new things. I think they deserve to learn new things.

Regardless of their age or their status as readers and writers, children also deserve to participate actively in conversations that let them build language muscles and connect to their peers and teachers in a joyful way. Read alouds are the perfect venue for such knowledge-building, for language development and use, and for building the authentic connections that transform groups of children into communities of readers and writers. But not your grandmother's read alouds! You will see that the authors of this text want read alouds to be instructive, interactive, and responsive. In my experience, that is easier said than done. It requires a model for planning and conducting read alouds grounded in research and informed by reason. You will find that model here, presented by authors who know research and know classrooms.

I have made the read aloud argument in professional development for many years, not always successfully. One of the hardest hurdles I have faced is that many teachers see their very traditional read alouds as already consistent with the research and vision that drive this text. Lisa Hammett Price and Barbara A. Bradley include realistic classroom dialogue to compare and contrast, inviting teachers to see the nuanced differences in practice that are required to make the best use of read aloud time. Their argument is reasoned and reasonable. It will hold water in the limited-resource system that constitutes the current English Language Arts block. They construct clear and accessible definitions of terms and real-life labels. My own favorite was this one: Think about your student's understanding, evidenced in discussion: Do you want to help a little, help a lot, or raise the bar?

The structure of the text, with separate chapters for each, has real potential to engender change. Many teachers are including more informational texts in their repertoire, but they may not understand that genre features present instructional opportunities. Comparing and contrasting the read aloud model across Chapters 5 through 8 will help teachers deepen their understanding of genre differences and better appreciate the need for genre diversity. Differences in craft and structure by genre are easily lost in the weeds; here they are presented clearly and with high-utility activities.

Another feature of this text that impressed me was attention to the realities of classroom organization. You will find realistic anchor charts, ones that I can imagine being posted immediately, specifically organized by the challenges that teachers are facing right now. How can my read alouds target key ideas and details? What about craft and structure? How can I use read alouds to scaffold the integration of knowledge and ideas that students will be asked to do in their own reading as they move into upper elementary grades? I know that I am going to use their examples in my work.

When university folk talk about the role of children's books in early primary classrooms, we run the risk of dividing ourselves into warring camps. One camp might argue that books are artistic creations to be enjoyed in whole. The other might claim that books are opportunities to meet very specific skill-oriented goals. Price and Bradley are more nimble than most. They walk the tightrope between the holistic traditions of early childhood and the isolated attention to skill-building that will enable more and more of us to welcome the demands of new standards. They present realistic routines for both challenging all students and accommodating those who need additional support. They also view the new emphasis on text complexity and text variety as an opportunity for children, rather than a punishment. I agree wholeheartedly. This book is a great read, filled with raise-the-bar opportunities for teaching and learning with literature, information text, poetry, and ebooks. If you choose to teach like this, children won't say they didn't learn anything in school today.

—Sharon Walpole, Ph.D., professor, University of Delaware

Preface

Each year, teachers have the opportunity to introduce young students to many exciting books. These include the ever-growing number of high-quality new releases, as well as classics like *The Very Hungry Caterpillar* (Carle, 1969), *Where the Wild Things Are* (Sendak, 1963), and *Alexander and the Terrible, Horrible, No Good, Very Bad Day* (Viorst, 1987). As teachers, we read to students for many different reasons: to stimulate their imagination, to show them the world outside the classroom walls, to share our beliefs and values, and to instill the joy of reading good books. While these reasons will never change, and should not change, reading aloud to young students plays another important role in children's lives: It helps to build a strong foundation for literacy that contributes to academic success. Teachers know this, and we have been choosing books and reading aloud to support early literacy for years.

In the past few decades, there has been a shift from read alouds primarily for entertainment purposes to read alouds used intentionally to foster students' literacy skills. For example, teachers have been encouraged to use books that contain rhyming and alliteration in order to teach phonological awareness. Teachers have been encouraged to select and teach specific vocabulary from books so that students can learn words not typically heard in daily conversations. Teachers have been encouraged to talk about the author and illustrator, to make print references to teach students concepts about print, and to focus on letters and the sounds they represent. The intent of such recommendations has been to recruit classroom read alouds to help achieve the national educational agenda of teaching all students to read on grade level by 3rd grade (No Child Left Behind Act of 2001).

However, focusing so much attention on teaching students skills that will support decoding during read alouds has had unexpected ramifications. Such emphasis on teaching the foundations for decoding has meant less attention on creating rich oral language interactions around books that help students develop the ability to comprehend and build knowledge through the reading of text. The Common Core State Standards (CCSS) for English Language Arts (National Governors Association Center for Best Practices [NGA] & Council of Chief State School Officers [CCSSO], 2010) changed the playing field for teachers and students by elevating the expectations for students to develop language and literacy skills necessary for the acquisition of deep disciplinary knowledge. While the need to learn basic decoding skills remains important, for obvious reasons, students will need to learn to read, think, and talk about complex texts in literature, science, social studies, history, and technical subjects. Therefore, even before students are capable of independently reading those complex texts, they need to have exposure to such texts, along with opportunities to learn strategies for comprehending and talking about the content in sophisticated ways.

There are five ways that the CCSS change the playing field in English Language Arts.

1. ***The CCSS focus on reading, writing, listening, speaking, and language as part of an integrated model of literacy.*** While the CCSS have separate standards for each of these areas, it recognizes that these processes are interrelated and should be taught in an integrated manner. Therefore, as students read or listen to text read aloud, they are expected to have opportunities to engage in both oral and written responses. Further, students' responses should demonstrate that they are thinking critically, solving problems, and connecting their ideas with those of their peers. Thus, the CCSS will require that students become proficient at using an academic language *register*, or "academic talk" (van Kleeck, 2014). Compared with social language or "casual talk," academic talk is characterized by greater formality, greater teacher control over topics, an expectation for precise vocabulary and complex grammar, and greater demands for high-level reasoning. Although many students come to school with a solid foundation in academic talk, other students may come to school needing teachers to help them learn this register. Therefore, it is important that we have methods for teaching students this register more explicitly than we have done in the past.

2. ***The CCSS necessitate the use of complex texts within the grade level.*** Previous standards specified what students needed to do, but did not specify text complexity. But we know that, for example, making inferences within a text that is easy differs from making inferences within a text that is challenging. Thus, the CCSS expect all students to interact with complex texts appropriate for their grade level. For students who are not yet proficient readers, this means listening to complex texts that are read aloud to them. While reading aloud to students is not a new practice, reading complex texts aloud might be, particularly with younger students. In addition to challenging students' listening comprehension, these complex texts are expected to encourage high-level thinking and discussions. For example, students will be expected to discuss, or write about, differences in points of view or to compare and contrast different texts. In order for students to participate successfully in such high-level discussions, they will need instructional support and encouragement from their teachers.

3. ***The CCSS expect students to read text closely and provide textual evidence.*** Close reading is defined as "an instructional routine in which students critically examine a text, especially through repeated readings . . . [and it] invites students to examine the deep structures of a piece of text" (Fisher & Frey, 2012, p. 179). So rather than relying primarily on their background knowledge, students will be expected to, for example, identify the key ideas and details and cite evidence from the text to support their conclusions. The goal is to shift students' attention away from relying on background knowledge or making personal connections to the text, and instead emphasize that readers need to *"stay within the four corners of the text"* (Serafini, 2013, p. 230). Although background knowledge and personal connections can aid in the comprehension of a text, students need to be aware of what the text actually says!

4. ***The CCSS encourage building disciplinary knowledge through informational texts.*** To build a foundation for college and career readiness, the CCSS indicate that students should read widely and deeply across a range of literary and informational texts. Thus, there will be a greater emphasis on reading texts in areas such as social studies and science. Those texts will be used to build the background knowledge needed to read complex informational texts with comprehension, as well as to engage in writing, speaking, and listening activities in the content areas. To help students develop this rich content knowledge, teachers can intentionally and coherently integrate informational texts into their curriculum, beginning in the early grades, and teach students how to extract and comprehend the information those texts contain.

5. ***The CCSS encourage shared responsibility for meeting the needs of diverse learners.*** In order for *all* students to achieve high academic standards, teachers and specialists will need to work together to provide high-quality research-based instruction, as well as individualized support and accommodations. While the CCSS do recognize that English language learners (ELLs) and students with disabilities have unique learning needs, it states that by diagnosing students' instructional needs, adjusting instruction, and monitoring student progress, all students can and should be expected to meet high academic standards. For students with disabilities, this may include instructional accommodations, including those based on the principles of Universal Design for Learning (UDL), or the use of assistive technology that supports better access to the general education curriculum. To support ELLs, students need teachers and support staff who are well prepared and who immerse students in literacy-rich environments with a variety of language experiences. They need to develop English skills while participating in grade-level coursework. Teachers can provide instruction that builds on ELLs' first language and literacy knowledge to support their developing English

language and literacy skills. The fact is that all students benefit when we tap into personal interests in order to motivate students, when we provide input using a variety of modalities (e.g., auditory, visual, perceptual), and when we accept a range of methods of output (e.g., speech, physical actions, writing or drawing) (Meyer, Rose, & Gordon, 2013).

With these changes in expectations, teachers will need instructional practices that can help students achieve them. Classroom read alouds provide a unique instructional setting for achieving such high academic standards. In fact, the CCSS identify read alouds as an instructional tool, and they provide specific recommendations for teachers regarding choosing and using texts. The CCSS emphasize literacy learning within the context of disciplinary content, and this will necessitate a wider scope of books selected for read alouds.

Over a decade ago, researchers revealed that storybooks were the predominant genre in preschool and elementary grade classrooms (Duke, 2000). Although progress has been made to integrate more informational texts into classrooms, there is still evidence that teachers find them difficult to read aloud (Price, Bradley, & Smith, 2012; Yopp & Yopp, 2006). Further, teachers tend to read storybooks and information books in similar ways, rather than maximizing the instructional possibilities of different genres (Price & Bradley, 2009). In classrooms where students are expected to read, think, and talk about complex texts in sophisticated ways, using a range of children's book genres will become a necessity rather than a luxury, and we will need to reconsider how we use different genres for our instructional purposes.

Although the CCSS guide kindergarten through Grade 12 education and are not inclusive of preschool education, preschool teachers already use read alouds as a common instructional practice. Consequently, preschool teachers are in a good position to develop our youngest students' early literacy, oral language, conceptual knowledge, and cognitive skills in ways that prepare them to meet the expectations of the CCSS. In fact, when we look at preschool state standards, we see many of the same types of expectations as are included in the CCSS, albeit at an earlier point in development. Therefore, preschool teachers have an opportunity to reflect on their curriculum and instructional practices so that they can help young students successfully transition into elementary school (National Association for the Education of Young Children, 2011; van Kleeck, 2008). Such an opportunity does not imply that preschool teachers should feel pressure to make preschool more academic and restrictive (Halpren, 2013). On the contrary, the emphasis in preschool remains teaching the "whole child" and providing a variety of purposeful experiences for young children. However, because reading aloud is a common instructional practice in preschool (van Kleeck, Stahl, & Bauer, 2003), we intentionally include this age group as part of the focus in this book.

We wrote this book because we have spent years reading books with students and researching read alouds. We have learned from teachers and students about the factors that help and hinder successful read alouds, and more specifically the factors that help and hinder the integration of different genres into the classroom (Bradley & Price, 2011). From these experiences, we have honed practical methods for how to help teachers achieve highly successful read alouds that can support students' achievement of the skills expected by the CCSS.

We agree with those who recommend making read alouds highly interactive; they suggest that teachers ask questions and engage students in conversation about the text during the read aloud. We believe, however, that teachers can achieve the lofty goals of the CCSS only if interactive read alouds include planned opportunities to think and talk at high levels of cognitive thinking, and if teachers become highly responsive to the students' verbal contributions. The interaction around the text needs to support and guide students to achieve greater levels of thinking, comprehension, and verbal expression. Therefore, in this book, we describe methods (1) to create *responsive* interactive read alouds, and (2) to use text genre strategically for instruction. Our target audience is classroom teachers and other specialists who use read alouds with students, including reading specialists, speech-language pathologists, and teachers of students who speak other languages.

The book is designed to be practical and user-friendly, a book that teachers will refer to often while planning read alouds and reflecting on responsive scaffolding. We start in Chapter 1 by providing a rationale for reading aloud to students and describing how reading different genres creates unique interactions and learning opportunities for students. In Chapter 2, we explore what we believe is often the missing ingredient in a read aloud—teacher responsiveness. Instead of suggesting a list of specific prompts to use, we suggest developing a responsive style of interacting as a first step to increasing the quality of interactions during alouds. Then in Chapter 3 we describe three types of scaffolding strategies teachers can provide in order to be highly responsive during a read aloud. These include High-Support Strategies, Low-Support Strategies, and Raise-the-Bar Strategies. By listening carefully and evaluating the content and language in students' contributions, teachers can provide tailored support when students are struggling, or raise the bar when students are ready for greater challenges. Chapter 4 continues this discussion by providing examples of teachers using the strategies during read alouds.

At that point, we shift gears to focus on text genre. Specifically, we provide guidance for using literature (Chapter 5), informational text (Chapter 6), poetry (Chapter 7), and digital texts (Chapter 8). Within each chapter we describe the benefits and challenges of that genre, and ways to plan effectively when using that genre. In each of those chapters, we suggest a variety of anchor charts and activities that can be used before, during, or after a read aloud to support specific Common Core standards. Throughout the book, we suggest ways to meet the needs of students with learning differences, including students with identified disabilities and ELLs. However, in Chapter 9, we describe additional structural, textual, and interactional accommodations to further support these students.

Throughout the book, we include teacher–student interactions taken from our research studies, illustrating student talk during read alouds and the teacher support that helped them achieve more than they could independently. We also provide visual examples of anchor charts, suggest specific children's books to use, and provide links to available Internet resources. Our hope is that teachers and other educators take read alouds in the classroom to the next level and experience the amazing discussions that can occur in the context of a good book.

CHAPTER 1

Why Reading Aloud Is Important

Imagine this scenario upon walking into a kindergarten classroom:

The teacher is sitting on a chair at the front of the classroom with a storybook held up. She is reading the words with animation and uses different voices for various characters. There are 20 students sitting or lying on the carpet in front of her, their eyes glued to the colorful pages of the book. They laugh and make comments, and the teacher responds briefly. A few students wiggle around and the teacher uses a gesture to get them back on their spots, but never veers away from reading the text. At the end of the story, a handful of students start talking at once, asking questions or noting something funny in the story. The teacher capitalizes on the energy, getting the students engaged in a short discussion about the problem the main character faced and how it was resolved. Before the students lose interest, the read aloud ends and students move to the next part of their school day.

Such a scene is common in preschool and early elementary school classrooms in the United States. Reading aloud creates an opportunity for teachers and students to share the pleasure of reading, experience the excitement of a good story, and wonder about the world around us. As teachers, we believe that it promotes a love of books and an interest in reading. However, we also know that reading aloud is an important instructional practice.

WHY READING ALOUD MATTERS

What may not be visible from the scene described above is what students are learning from the activity. Reading aloud certainly helps to motivate students to want to read (Klesius & Griffith, 1996). But evidence also shows that reading aloud supports development of skills including

- Listening comprehension (Morrow & Gambrell, 2002)
- Vocabulary and concept knowledge (Neuman & Dwyer, 2011; Neuman, Newman, & Dwyer, 2011)
- Receptive and expressive language skills (Gerde & Powell, 2009; Hargrave & Sénéchal, 2000)

- Awareness of text structures such as story schema (van den Broek, 2001)
- Sensitivity to the linguistic and organizational structures of books (Duke & Kays, 1998)
- Print awareness (Pullen & Justice, 2003)
- Word recognition skills (Stahl, 2003)
- Monitoring comprehension and making corrections while reading (Smolkin & Donovan, 2001)
- Understanding how voice or intonation can change meaning (Harste, Woodward, & Burke, 1984)

Given such research findings, it is hard not to believe that reading aloud is a pivotal instructional activity. However, despite the fact that read alouds have merit, there is also evidence that when read alouds limit the time students actually practice reading with an adult or reading on their own, students' reading achievement can suffer (Meyer, Stahl, Wardrop, & Linn, 1994). Therefore, reading aloud should not supplant reading instruction or students' opportunities to engage in guided or independent reading.

How can we reconcile the research that shows important benefits of reading aloud in the classroom with the research that cautions us not to let reading aloud overtake actual reading instruction? With the CCSS entering the scene, with their much higher expectations for student achievement, does reading aloud still warrant a place in the instructional scene for young students in preschool through 2nd grade? The answer to that question is a resounding *yes*, and here are three reasons why.

Reading Aloud Provides Exposure to Complex Texts Before Students Are Capable of Reading Those Texts Independently

In the early grades, when students are still learning how to read, they will need texts that include features such as decodable words and predictable language. Yet students eventually need to be able to read and comprehend texts that are much more complex. This has always been true; however, the CCSS up the ante by requiring texts that are more complex than previous educational standards and stipulating that teachers begin to incorporate complex texts earlier. Students need such early exposure to complex texts in order to develop the language and cognitive skills needed for independent text comprehension when they are in fact readers. To accomplish this, students need thoughtful instruction early on that lays a foundation for comprehension of those complex texts.

Reading aloud is an important instructional activity for achieving this goal because teachers can model the kinds of comprehension strategies students will need to use later when they read independently. However, simply reading complex texts aloud and making a few comments will not be sufficient. In this book, we describe methods for reading aloud that help teachers use and teach comprehension strategies so that students can comprehend complex texts before they are capable of reading them independently.

Reading Aloud Provides Opportunities for Active Participation and Collaboration with Peers

Oral language abilities provide a foundation for academic success. Oral language includes both the expressive domain (speaking) and receptive domain (listening). In terms of expressive language, the CCSS expect students in kindergarten through 2nd grade to speak in well-formulated sentences that are relevant to the content and social nature of the conversation. In terms of receptive language, students need to demonstrate listening skills by asking and answering questions that are relevant to a text or topic of discussion. They must understand what others have said about the topic so that their own verbal contributions build on previous ideas. In order to achieve these receptive and expressive language skills, teachers can help students collaborate verbally within discussions about a text. Discussions must go beyond simply eliciting a few answers to questions during or after reading aloud. Rather, they need to involve multiple students and multiple turns on topic, with students building on what others have said already. Further, the content of the talk needs to show students' ability to use an academic language register, including use of diverse and sophisticated vocabulary, complex and more formal grammar, and explanation of abstract concepts.

Although speaking and listening can and should be addressed all day long in the classroom, the activity of reading books aloud is particularly well suited for focusing on language. For one, the grammar and vocabulary contained in books are more sophisticated than that typically found in conversational language. Thus, the text itself already provides a model of academic language. In addition, the activity can involve much more than a teacher reading the text aloud. Teachers ask questions that stimulate discussion, and they follow up on students' questions and comments in responsive ways that help to expand students' language skills and use of an academic register. In this book, we describe methods teachers can use to help students actively participate, collaborate with peers, and make connections across curricular topics while discussing the content presented in a book.

Reading Aloud Provides Opportunities to Think and Speak at High Levels of Cognitive Thinking

Clearly, students with solid basic language skills are in a better position to do well academically. However, beyond basic language skills, they need to learn to use language to engage in higher levels of cognitive thinking. This type of language has also been called decontextualized language, abstract language, or inferential language (for discussion, see van Kleeck, 2014). Language at high levels of cognitive thinking includes analyzing, comparing, contrasting, predicting, evaluating, judging, or drawing conclusions. Students who are skilled at using language at high levels of cognitive thinking perform better on measures of reading comprehension, and they achieve more academically.

One hallmark of the CCSS is teaching students to engage in "close, attentive reading" that leads to high levels of comprehension of the complex texts they are reading. To achieve this, students must learn to listen or read critically in order to determine what a text says, make logical inferences, and analyze a text's craft and structure to interpret the text's meaning and tone. Furthermore, students need to be capable of evaluating the effectiveness or value of a text. They need to use the information and ideas from a text as evidence to support their own responses. Reaching these higher levels of cognitive thinking takes years to achieve and, therefore, the CCSS emphasize learning that builds over time. Students are expected to apply their developing knowledge and skills rather than just recite basic facts or low-level content. If students are to achieve such lofty goals for reading comprehension in the later grades, it is clear that this effort must begin in the early grades.

Reading aloud is one method for reaching these high levels of cognitive thinking. In fact, reading aloud is one of the activities most likely to include discussion at high levels of cognitive thinking compared with the huge amount of procedural and management talk in classrooms, which tends to be at low levels of cognitive thinking (Kontos & Wilcox-Herzog, 1997). The CCSS include recommendations for reading aloud to students because participating in rich conversations with an adult helps students to develop verbal language and listening skills as well as cognitive skills and concept knowledge (NGA & CCSSO, 2010).

For students to achieve the goals set by the CCSS, teachers need to choose books wisely and have a plan for read alouds so that the interaction can reach higher levels, rather than simply picking a book off the shelf and hoping that students make connections or think deeply about it. In this book, we describe methods to create read alouds that are

1. Instructive (they include both low and high levels)
2. Interactive (they give students the opportunity to practice language at low and high levels)
3. Responsive (teachers provide tailored support to scaffold low and high levels of language and thinking)

In addition, we show how teachers can use these methods across three different genres of text in order to achieve different instructional purposes.

WHY TEXT GENRE MATTERS

In the scenario we described earlier, students were captivated while listening to their teacher read a storybook aloud. Let's consider another scenario:

The same kindergarten teacher is sitting on a chair at the front of the classroom with an informational book held up. She is reading the words with wonder and curiosity. There are 20 students sitting or lying on the carpet in front of her, eyes glued to the colorful pages of the book. They make connections to the content; some comments are on topic while others are tangential, but the teacher acknowledges each contribution. She focuses students' attention on a particular diagram, explaining it. When they appear confused or lose focus, the teacher draws students' attention to the bright photographs, rereads a bit of text, or connects the information to other activities they have done in class in order to help them to understand the information. A few students wiggle around and the teacher gets them to come up and point to something on the pages, re-engaging them in the topic. After a few minutes, the teacher reaches a planned stopping point in the book. The teacher helps the students identify what new information they learned about the topic and how it relates to what they already know. Before the students start to lose focus, the teacher ends the read aloud.

These students are all interested in the information book, asking questions and wanting to know more about the topic. In fact, during informational text read alouds, teachers and students both engage in more talk beyond the text than they typically do with storybooks (Price et al., 2012). Further, teachers report that students are equally attentive, and they enjoy both storybook and informational book read alouds. Primary grade teachers report that providing a variety of informational texts is motivating and allows students to pursue their own interests (Maloch, 2008).

Yet the reality is that storybooks continue to be the most prevalent text genre read aloud in preschool and early elementary classrooms. While the evidence is clear that reading storybooks aloud supports children's language and early literacy development (e.g., van Kleeck et al., 2003; Wasik, Bond, & Hindman, 2006), other genres like informational texts and poetry have usefulness and merit for read alouds in the classroom, too. Why exactly does it matter if teachers read a variety of genres of text? We discuss two reasons for why genre matters.

Different Genres of Text Create Different Interactions and Different Instructional Opportunities

When a teacher reads aloud with students, the center of everyone's attention is the book itself. The teacher reads the text in the book, points to the illustrations, and talks about the topic of the book. The text in the book, and the illustrations and other visual features, are important parts of the equation during a read aloud. They guide what teachers and students do and say during the activity. For too long, we have ignored the effects of the book itself, instead focusing on the students and the reader. Yet the text affects the language students are exposed to and the language they use during the activity. Therefore, genre affects the instructional quality of the talk (for a discussion, see van Kleeck, 2003).

How genre affects talk: Storybooks and informational texts. How exactly does genre affect the talk? It affects how much teachers and students talk, when that talk occurs (before, during, or after reading), the grammatical complexity of the talk, and the cognitive level of the talk. When teachers and students interact around a storybook, talk usually occurs before and after reading, with some talk during the read aloud. However, too much talk during the read aloud disrupts the narrative flow and may impede students' comprehension of the text. Therefore, many teachers try to read the text without lengthy discussions, at least the first time they read it, and save discussions for after reading. When reading stories, there tends to be less talk overall compared with informational text read alouds (even when the books are about the same length). In addition, the content of the talk tends to be about characters' actions or the content of illustrations, which are at low levels of cognitive thinking. Talk at high levels of cognitive thinking occurs too, but less often. However, storybooks offer a good context for making inferences about characters' feelings and intentions, making predictions about what might happen next, or making experiential and text-to-text connections.

The talk during informational text read alouds differs from storybooks in that there is considerably more talk overall, and talk occurs before, during, and after reading. Unlike the text structure of storybooks, the text structure of informational texts usually allows for more talk during the read aloud. In fact, talk during the read aloud likely helps students' comprehension rather than hindering it. Informational texts include technical vocabulary and concepts that often become the topic of discussion. Students tend to initiate many more questions and comments during informational text read alouds, and that adds to the amount of talk that occurs overall. There is a greater balance between low and high levels of cognitive thinking during informational text reading. Talk at low levels tends to include drawing attention to details in illustrations or photographs, labeling items, or describing attributes or characteristics.

Informational texts also offer a good context for talk at high levels, although the types differ compared with storybook reading. Talk at high levels tends to include

- Summarizing
- Making comparisons
- Explaining a concept
- Defining words
- Making experiential, text-to-text, and text-to-world connections

Talk during informational texts also includes discussions about text features such as the table of contents, glossary, and diagrams with labels. For example, Gail Gibbons's (1999) informational book on bats includes a diagram to scale showing the length of a bat's wingspan compared with the length of its body. Instructive diagrams and other text features stimulate comments and questions from students, and teachers are able to use diagrams to aid in explaining the content or answering students' questions. Informational text structures often allow teachers to choose what to read and what to omit. Such flexibility helps keep the read aloud to a reasonable length of time, while still allowing discussion. Therefore, teachers can make decisions judiciously about what parts of the text to read in order to preserve the richness of informational text while also achieving their learning objectives and controlling the duration of the read aloud.

How genre affects talk: Poetry. Teachers read all the text in poetry; the text structure demands it. The talk during poetry read alouds differs from that during storybooks and informational texts. The majority of talk occurs before and after reading; poems need to be read without interruption in order to appreciate their use of language, rhythm, rhyme, meter, pattern, and structure. Poems include many opportunities for teaching imagery, figurative language, and sophisticated vocabulary. Talk at low levels of cognitive thinking tends to include checking basic understanding of the language, drawing attention to rhythm and rhyme, or supporting visualization. Poetry offers a good context for talk at high levels of cognitive thinking, but again that differs compared with storybook and informational text reading. Poetry offers opportunities for defining words, discussing synonyms, making inferences, providing explanations of concepts, eliciting opinions, describing mood and feelings conveyed by the poem, or analyzing the author's choice of words or language. Talk also tends to be about poetic devices and qualities such as rhyme, alliteration, visual structure, and forms.

Differences in talk matter. It is clear that text genre changes what teachers and students do and say during the activity. But why do these differences in the talk matter? They matter because the interactions influence what students learn from the activity. First, students who hear and engage in more talk at higher levels of cognitive thinking achieve better language and literacy skills

(Taylor, Pearson, Peterson, & Rodriquez, 2002). Each genre of text offers opportunities for talk at high levels of cognitive thinking. If we can make all read alouds more interactive, and also increase the amount of talk at higher levels of cognitive thinking, then those read alouds can contribute more to students' long-term language and literacy development. In this book, we will talk about practical ways to increase the interactive nature of read alouds across storybooks, informational books, and poetry, and how to use these genres to achieve discussions that reach high levels of cognitive thinking.

Second, students learn different language features from various genres of book. For example, when students retell familiar storybooks and informational books, they use the language features specific to each genre in their retellings (Bradley & Price, 2011). When retelling a story, they use past tense verbs, verbs that refer to characters' thoughts and intentions (e.g., "thought," "wanted," "wondered"), coordinating conjunctions (e.g., "and," "but"), complex grammar, and references to specific characters by name and later with appropriate pronouns (e.g., "Grace" and later "she"). When retelling an informational text, students use present tense verbs, reference classes or categories (e.g., "squirrels" rather than "the squirrel"), and use plural pronouns (e.g., "squirrels" and later "they"). In each genre, they use vocabulary that is specific to that genre and topic. Similarly, poetry reading teaches students about other language features such as rhythm, rhyme, patterns, alliteration, imagery, figurative language, and moods or feelings conveyed through word choices.

In short, there are benefits to language and literacy learning when we read a variety of text genres with students. In fact, we can intentionally use different genres to serve different instructional purposes required by the standards for our grade level. In this book, we will discuss methods for intentionally exploiting the benefits of each genre through read alouds.

Different Disciplines Rely on Different Genres of Text

The CCSS focus on building students' discipline-specific knowledge through reading and writing, and different disciplines rely on different genres. For example, English language arts include narratives, fables, fantasy, folktales, drama, picture books, novels, and poetry. Many of these genres include narrative features such as characters, setting, initiating event, character goals, attempts to achieve those goals, and a final outcome. Science relies on concept books, procedural how-to texts, and expository texts explaining the physical and biological world. Science texts tend to include descriptions and comparisons, as well as visual features such as diagrams and graphs. History and social studies texts are informational but may include features of narratives as they present information in a chronological or sequential order. That is, they might explain historical events in a storylike manner. They also may include visual features such as maps and timelines.

As students read, or listen to, different genres to gain content knowledge, they must become aware of how different text structures and features convey information. Not only will this help them to understand the content, but also we expect students to use these text structures and features in their own writing. We can prepare students for the upper elementary grades by exposing them to different genres in preschool and the primary grades and by helping them to understand and use features of various genres in their own writing (for example, see Moline, 2011). In this book, we will discuss how to use genre intentionally in the early grades to lay the foundation for later success.

COMMON MISCONCEPTIONS ABOUT READING ALOUD

Storybooks have been the foundation of read alouds for many years. Teachers have developed their read aloud techniques and honed their skills using stories as the context. Because of this, features of storybook reading tend to prevail when teachers read informational texts and poetry. The storybook skill set tends to be the framework for all other read alouds, despite differences in text structure, visual and text features, and the different opportunities that various genres provide. Consequently, misconceptions about reading aloud continue to prevail, and they can limit the instructional potential of read alouds in the classroom. Four misconceptions continue to exist.

Misconception 1:
Teachers Can Read Books the Same Way No Matter What the Genre

One misconception about reading aloud is that we can approach all books the same way, using the same routines, same behavior management strategies, and same types of talk. The reality is that the same routines and strategies do not work well across all text genres, and we are setting ourselves up for trouble when we fail to alter our approach accordingly. Styles of reading aloud vary across teachers (Dickinson & Smith, 1991; Martinez & Teale, 1993), and there is no one right way to read aloud or one approach that will foster learning in all students. However, teachers tend to use the same style across text genres (Price et al., 2012). Specifically, teachers tend to rely on the same types of talk, use the same group size, and have the same expectations for when and how students should participate (e.g., calling out versus hand-raising) during the read aloud. Yet using the same strategies and having the same expectations regardless of genre can result in lost learning opportunities, or worse, more behavioral challenges, during the activity. We describe in this book the benefits of considering text genre when making decisions regarding group size, participation routines, and methods for initiating discussion.

Misconception 2:
We Need to Read Books from Cover to Cover

Storybooks are best read in their entirety either in one sitting, or sequentially over multiple sessions (as with chapter books). Because of this, teachers understandably may have the perception that we need to read all the text from beginning to end. However, this is not the case for every genre. Yes, for storybooks it is helpful to read the text through fully and sequentially; students need to follow key events and details of stories in order to comprehend them. Similarly, it is best to read an entire poem so that students can appreciate the elements of poetry such as rhythm, rhyme, mood, and tone. In fact, poems need to be read multiple times in order for students to appreciate all these features. Conversely, informational text may or may not necessarily need to be read all in one sitting or in order or even in its entirety. For example, in an expository text describing features of bats (e.g., *Time for Kids: Bats!*, by Iorio, 2005), it is possible to read only several pages aloud so that students learn certain facts about bats that achieve the learning objectives. It is not necessary to read the entire book, because comprehending the target information is not dependent upon hearing other information in the text. All informational texts are not the same, however. If reading a procedural text describing the steps in making crayons (e.g., *From Wax to Crayon*, by Forman, 1997), it is necessary to read from the beginning and in sequential order. As teachers, we have to make decisions regarding how much of a text is necessary for comprehension, and more specifically, for our instructional purposes. We describe in this book how to choose texts and portions of texts to meet specific instructional purposes.

Misconception 3:
Our Students Will Get Bored if We Read a Book More Than Once or Twice

Teachers tend to read a book one time with students for a single purpose (Donovan, Milewicz, & Smolkin, 2003). They believe that students enjoy the book only during the first reading and may get bored if we read the same one again. Students show us, however, that this is not true. Our experience both personally and professionally has been that students want us to read the same books repeatedly. They ask us to read the same book over and over. With each successive reading, students begin to engage in different and more complex ways, and they enjoy the book more as they feel increasingly competent with the content. In the classroom, though, there has been concern that students are less engaged during repeated readings. This may be true when we read the book the same way every time (see misconception 1) or when there is not a clear purpose for each repeated reading. However, multiple readings support students learning, especially if we vary our interactions and expectations during each reading (see McGee & Schickedanz, 2007) and plan different instructional purposes for each separate read aloud.

There are a number of good reasons to read some texts repeatedly from an instructional standpoint as well. First, many students need more than one read aloud in order to comprehend the book content, retain it, and learn new vocabulary (Biemiller & Boote, 2006). This is especially true for ELLs (Barone & Xu, 2008) and students with language impairments (Kaderavek & Justice, 2002). Second, with each repeated reading, students can take on more responsibility for the read aloud. For example, McGee and Schickedanz (2007) describe different approaches for the first, second, and third read aloud of the same book, with increasing expectations for student participation. By the third reading, the teacher guides the students to reconstruct the story. Such an approach can be adapted for informational texts and poetry. Third, teachers can choose different instructional purposes for each repeated reading to help students achieve greater depth of knowledge. For example, with a story, the first reading could include a discussion of the problem the characters faced and how they solved them, the second reading could address the feelings of various characters and relating those to personal experiences, and the third could focus on how the story might change if the characters tried other methods to solve the problem. We describe in this book ways to achieve repeated readings in the classroom, how to use different types of talk across successive readings, and how to expect more from students with each reading of a text.

Misconception 4:
Asking a Few Good Questions and Making a Few Comments
During a Read Aloud Will Result in Learning from the Activity

Asking good instructional questions during a read aloud and making comments that support comprehension are both important, but they do not necessarily result in conversations that lead to content and language learning. We often see read alouds that include simple initiation-response-evaluation routines or a question followed by a few student responses. The talk does not reach the level of an instructional dialogue. The CCSS make it more important that teachers create instructional conversations about a text, engaging multiple students for multiple turns on a topic. Such conversations require first planning ways to initiate the dialogue. Second, and perhaps more importantly, such conversations require that teachers respond to students' contributions in ways that meet them where they are, scaffolding those students to higher levels of language skill and content knowledge. Teachers also can support students *more* by guiding their thinking and helping them craft their responses. Alternatively, teachers can support students *less* by encouraging them to elaborate or clarify. Or teachers can raise the bar in ways that require even deeper thinking and more complex language for those who need the challenge. In this book, we will discuss ways to scaffold student responses to provide high support, to back off using low support, or to raise the bar to push students who are ready for it.

SUMMARY

In this chapter, we identified three reasons why reading aloud to students matters. We also explored how reading different genres to students is important. Last, we reflected on common misconceptions about reading aloud to students and the evidence refuting those misconceptions. In short, reading aloud is important. Reading different genres aloud is important. While it can take time and practice to learn to read different genres with ease and confidence, in the end, our students will benefit from those efforts.

CHAPTER 2

Responsiveness:
The Missing Ingredient

Researchers and educators alike agree that read alouds need to include many opportunities for students to engage in rich discussion about the text. The recommendation is that teachers ask students questions, answer their queries, assist them in making sense of complex ideas, and encourage them to explain their thinking. There is consensus on the importance of interaction. Rich discussion during read alouds is the mechanism for increasing students' comprehension, verbal expression, vocabulary and content knowledge, and depth of thinking.

Many resources describe methods for achieving such interaction during a read aloud. They typically recommend that teachers do the following:

- Invite students to talk
- Ask wh- questions at both low and high levels of cognitive thinking
- Ask open-ended questions
- Praise students' contributions
- Provide feedback on students' contributions
- Help students correct misunderstandings
- Provide rich explanations of vocabulary
- Ask students to define words or provide definitions
- Elicit imitations of words or phrases
- Point to and label the illustrations
- Model our own thinking
- Ask students to explain their thinking
- Ask students to make predictions and inferences
- Allow wait time
- Repeat the student's ideas and expand their sentences
- Relate the text to students' life experiences
- Relate the text to other texts the students know

We agree with everything on this list, and we have taught inservice and preservice teachers to use these types of strategies to achieve an interactive read aloud. Despite such lists of ways to create interactive read alouds, the quality of interaction during the activity continues to vary widely across teachers. For example, we continue to see read alouds that follow a traditional pattern of interaction that looks like this:

The teacher introduces the text by reading the title and author and illustrator names. The teacher asks what an author or illustrator does. Then the teacher asks students to predict what the text might be about. The teacher calls on two or three students to share their predictions. The focus is typically on the cover illustration as a means for generating predictions, and predictions tend to be relatively shallow. The teacher accepts all student ideas without question, saying, "Maybe that's what the book will be about," or "Maybe that will happen—let's read it and see." The teacher does this even when the students' prediction is relatively weak. Then the teacher proceeds to read the text. Students sit and listen; the teacher manages behavior as needed (e.g., "Charlie, sit on your bottom in your chair"; "Susan, go get a tissue and wash your hands"; "Wait until I finish reading"). While reading, the teacher occasionally asks a question or points to an illustration. Interactions typically last one to three turns and involve a question, one or two answers to that question, and an evaluation of whether those answers were correct; the typical initiation-response-evaluation format. Occasionally the teacher asks a student to clarify what he or she means before proceeding. The teacher answers some students' questions when they are interesting, but hushes other students who interject questions, telling them to wait. The teacher provides quick definitions for a few unfamiliar words while reading to make sure students know what those words mean. When a student displays a misunderstanding about the text or struggles to formulate her or his idea, the teacher corrects the student with a brief explanation and then moves on.

Many teachers recognize that this pattern is less than ideal and work toward changing it. They try to integrate more of the strategies on the list above into their read alouds. We have used a list similar to the one above to provide evaluations of read alouds by checking off the strategies that teachers use. Many teachers demonstrate the use of all those strategies, not necessarily all within the same read aloud but at least over the course of several. Clearly, they have all these strategies in their repertoire. Yet their read alouds still fail to reach the level of rich discussion they are striving for. Why does this continue to be the prevailing style of interaction during read alouds? Why does it continue to be the style even after the teacher works to change it?

The answer is that we have all focused on a list of strategies as though it is a checklist, assuming that if we do those things during a read aloud, we will achieve rich discussion and deep learning. However, by focusing too much on what we need to *do* during the read aloud, we have created two problems. First, we have continued to reinforce a pattern of teacher-student interaction that students have grown to expect in the classroom; that is, that the teacher will ask questions, a student will answer, and the teacher will evaluate the student's response. Students have learned to expect this initiation-response-evaluation sequence, and they wait for teachers to drive the conversation. Therefore, students influence teachers to continue using this style.

Second, focusing on what we need to *do* during the read aloud results in a failure to listen carefully to students' responses and to use what they say as the foundation for what we do next. The goal is to jointly construct meaning during a read aloud; however, to do that requires actively listening to what students say and then responding in ways that help them construct meaning at the highest level they can achieve.

In short, RESPONSIVENESS *is a key ingredient of an effective interactive read aloud.* Responsiveness can solve both of the problems described. Our goal is to learn how to provide support or scaffolding when students are struggling and to raise the bar when students are ready for a challenge. While the list of strategies above can help accomplish these goals, those strategies will be successful only when we evaluate the content and language in students' contributions and tailor what we do in ways that are responsive to them. Further, responsiveness shows students that we are truly listening to what they have to say, not simply looking for one predetermined answer. When we are responsive to students' contributions, the talk can move away from an initiation-response-evaluation sequence toward true discussion and joint construction of meaning. Students learn to drive the talk, too, rather than passively waiting on teachers to do it for them.

We suggest two approaches for increasing responsiveness during read alouds. First, in this chapter, we discuss ways to adopt a responsive interaction style in the classroom in general. Learning to be responsive during a variety of activities in the classroom can build the skills needed to be responsive during read alouds. Next, in Chapter 3, we present a set of responsive-interactive scaffolding strategies to apply during read alouds specifically.

ADOPTING A RESPONSIVE INTERACTION STYLE IN THE CLASSROOM

Think about your classroom environment. Is it a place where students can ask questions and express ideas and opinions? Do you encourage your students to explore and consider new ideas? Do you acknowledge students' responses but then tell them the "right" answer? Consider the following scenarios. Which is most common in your classroom?

Scenario 1

Teacher: Where do the frogs go when it gets cold?
Anthony: They go hide themselves in the mud.
Teacher: That's right; frogs hibernate in the winter just like bears.
   (Teacher continues reading the text)

Scenario 2

Teacher: Where do the frogs go when it gets cold?

Lillian: They go hide themselves in the mud.

Teacher: Hmm. Why do you think frogs hide in the mud?

Isaac: To be warm.

Teacher: So when it's cold, frogs hide in the mud to stay warm. Tell me more about that.

Mila: The frogs stay under the mud all winter.

Teacher: Oh, so they hide in the mud to stay warm all winter long. There are other animals that hide away all winter too. Do you remember?

Mila: Bears.

Conner: Turtles.

Zoey: Cats.

Ryan: No they don't.

Teacher: Okay; bears and turtles do but cats don't. What is it called when animals do this?

Students: Hibernating!!

Teacher: Ah, you remember the word for it. They hibernate. Now frogs choose to hide in mud. Why is mud a good choice?

Isaac: Because it's warm.

Teacher: It's warm. (Waits)

Lucy: It's gooey.

Owen: No one can see them under there.

Teacher: Someone explain more about what Owen just said—no one can see them.

Aubrey: He don't want fish to see him because they might eat him.

Carter: It's like a predator.

Teacher: So frogs hide in the mud to stay warm but also to help protect themselves from predators like fish who might eat them. Wow. Okay. Listen to the next part of the text. It tells another reason why frogs hibernate in the mud.

Scenario 1 illustrates a *directive* approach, creating a culture where students expect us to ask factual questions and to tell them the "right" answers. One student's response need not be connected at all to another student's response.

Scenario 2 illustrates a *responsive* approach, encouraging students to say more and to grapple with ideas with our guidance. When we strive for a responsive style of interaction, we respond to a student's comment or question in order to encourage more elaboration and guide the student's thinking.

The type of style we adopt within our classroom will influence what happens during all activities, including read alouds. What we know is that there are benefits to a responsive style of interaction compared with a directive style. An adult who is responsive uses what students say to guide them to deeper connections and more complex thinking. Students show better language growth when the adults around them use a responsive style. This is true for students who are typically developing (Neuman & Gallagher, 1994) as well as for students with language or cognitive impairments (Dodici, Draper, & Peterson, 2003) and for ELLs (Gibbons, 2003). Therefore, teachers can support children's language development by adopting a responsive style of interaction in which they actively listen to students' questions and comments and make careful decisions when responding to help students clarify or extend their thinking. A responsive style is beneficial during interactive read alouds as well.

What does a responsive style of interaction look like? Let's look at another interaction that would be considered responsive to students' questions and comments. This excerpt is from a 1st-grade teacher reading with her students. The teacher's primary purpose during this read aloud session was to help students understand the difference between stories and nonfiction books (which she called "All About" books), and to notice text features in the nonfiction book. However, the teacher also wanted students to learn the content in the book. So, as the teacher is reading about where sharks live, a student asks her a question about a word she read.

Dominic: Why are they lurking?
Teacher: *Lurking* means they are being quiet and sneaky. So why do you think the shark is lurking?
Dominic: He's going to eat somebody!
Teacher: So the shark is lurking because it's going to eat something? We'll have to see what sharks eat.

The teacher then points out the next heading and reads the text about reef sharks. When she gets to the next section, the teacher asks a student about that heading.

Teacher: Chris, what do you think this section of the book will tell us? It's called, "On the Hunt."
Chris: Um, hunting for fish?
Teacher: About *me* hunting for fish?
Chris: No, about a shark hunting for fish.
Teacher: About a shark hunting for fish. How do you know that?
Chris: There's a shark chasing fish.
Teacher: There is a picture of a shark hunting for fish.

The teacher continues reading about how sharks track down their prey, when a student makes a comment about information in the book.

Sara: I didn't know that sharks could smell.

Teacher: I didn't know that either. What is something else we've learned about sharks so far?

Nolan: Sharks are scary.

Teacher: Okay, but what have you learned about sharks from this "All About" book or nonfiction book?

Nolan: It's not safe to swim in water with sharks.

Teacher: Okay, it's not safe to swim with sharks, but did the book tell us that or is that something that you already know?

Nolan: Already know it.

Teacher: So you're making that connection to the information. But did you learn something from this nonfiction book?

Nolan: If they don't keep swimming they'll sink.

Teacher: If they don't keep swimming, they'll sink. That's just such interesting information, isn't it? What else have we learned about sharks? Turn to your shoulder buddy and share something that you learned about sharks from the book.

Being responsive to students' contributions starts with being contingent. *Contingent* means that our talk depends on (or is contingent upon) students' talk. Thus, we follow a student's lead by talking about the same topic rather than changing the topic. We respond in a way that is sensitive to a student's needs and interests. Being responsive also means that we react quickly and we are genuine as we help the student to think about or develop a deeper understanding about the information at hand.

In the example, a student initiates interest in a particular statement in the book by asking why sharks are lurking. The teacher follows the child's lead. She decides that the student may be confused by the word "lurking" and provides a definition. Once the student has the definition, the teacher asks the student to answer his own question. The student responds by using a picture clue on the page. Rather than explaining at that moment why the sharks are lurking in the ocean, she reminds the students to pay attention to the text to learn the answer to that question.

After reading more text, the teacher asks a student to predict what the next section might be about based on its heading, "On the Hunt." One of her primary purposes for this read aloud is to help students understand informational text features like headings. While the student's response contains accurate content, it is a phrase rather than a full sentence and the student uses a question intonation. Therefore, the teacher asks for clarification, giving the student an opportunity to provide a more complete answer and with more confidence. Further, the teacher follows up by asking the student to provide evidence for his thinking, a hallmark of the CCSS.

At another point in the read aloud, a student makes a comment about interesting information in the book that was new to her. One of the teacher's instructional purposes is to teach students that nonfiction text gives us information and we can learn new things from it. She responds directly to the student's comment by admitting that she also did not know that piece of information, which is a community-building move. Although she is the teacher, she models that she is also a learner. She builds upon this by helping other students recognize the new information they have learned from this book.

In the exchange that follows, the teacher continues to use a responsive style of interaction, especially in how she deals with a student's response that is inaccurate. Specifically, when a student responds, "Sharks are scary," the teacher is responsive by acknowledging it ("Okay") and then providing scaffolding that supports the intent of the original question—what did students learn *from the text*. When the student provides another reasonable answer, but clearly not from the text, the teacher helps the student think about his response in light of her request to share what they learned from the text. She asks him if his knowledge about sharks came from the book or if it was something that he already knew. Once the student recognizes that he is using his prior knowledge to make a connection with the text, which is a comprehension strategy the class learned previously, then the student is able to provide information he learned from the text itself. In short, the teacher thinks carefully about the student's responses to identify a misunderstanding and provide tailored support. She also uses the student's responses to achieve the instructional intent of her original question to the class, "What is something else we've learned about sharks so far?" Finally, sensitive to the fact that she has a relatively lengthy exchange for a whole-class read aloud, she asks the students to "turn to your shoulder buddy and share something that you learned about sharks from the book." In doing so, all students have an opportunity to talk about what they have learned, and the teacher can quickly and easily evaluate their responses and provide more support to the buddy pairs if needed.

WHY IS RESPONSIVENESS EFFECTIVE?

Why does responsiveness help students to develop language and content knowledge? It works for three reasons. First, students are more likely to learn from talk about what they are already paying attention to and topics they are interested in. They are much more likely to respond on topic and imitate the language we use when it is contingent on their own talk. Imitating our model boosts their receptive and expressive language. Therefore, when it is possible, it helps to stay on the student's topic as long as we can, creating a multiple-turn interaction. Multiple-turn interactions are one expectation of the CCSS Speaking and Listening Standards. This does not mean, however, that when a student's comment is completely off topic we drop everything and follow that student down the rabbit hole! Off-topic comments need redirection. While the student's responses "Sharks are scary" and "It's not safe to swim in water with sharks" were not off topic, they didn't answer the teacher's question about what students had learned from the text. So, rather than accepting them, the teacher stayed true to her intent, helped the student become aware of prior knowledge compared with new knowledge gained from the text, and persisted until the student identified a new fact he had learned.

Second, responsive talk helps reduce the amount of information in a teacher's sentence that the student has to process (Proctor-Williams, Fey, & Frome Loeb, 2001). Because the teacher is using some of the same words that the student already used, it is easier for the student to recognize and learn the new bits of information that the teacher added to the sentence. This reduces the cognitive load and allows students to focus attention on new language, and therefore it is easier to learn.

Third, when we use a responsive style, students become more willing to participate verbally. When we are responsive, there are many right ways to participate, and therefore, students experience more success. That success bolsters their confidence and they become more willing to talk. This increased verbal participation has many benefits. More talk equals more practice with language and content knowledge. More talk results in more opportunities for teachers to scaffold. More frequent scaffolding, and specifically scaffolding that is better tailored to a student's needs, leads to greater learning for a student. Students' verbal contributions are a window into their understanding of content and their ability to use language. When students show us they are confused about the content, we can help lead them to understanding. When students make astute and interesting observations, we can raise the bar to help them achieve even more. But we need to hear their ideas and their language in order to know what support they need.

In contrast, when we use a directive style, we have one or two correct answers in mind; that is, we have an agenda that restricts how students can participate. Students learn quickly that we want a particular answer and we are not really interested in what they have to say. This tends to decrease students' willingness to talk, which also means fewer opportunities for the teacher to scaffold learning. Although a directive approach is detrimental for all students, it is more detrimental for students with language difficulties and for ELLs because these students are less likely to be persistent about talking in class. Thus, they get fewer opportunities to practice language and they receive less scaffolding and support. A responsive style works for students who are typically developing, but it is particularly important for students who are ELLs or who have learning differences (Barachetti & Lavelli, 2011; Lim & Cole, 2002). Therefore, adopting a responsive style in the classroom has particular benefits for those students who need the greatest support for language and content learning.

HOW TO BE RESPONSIVE

What can teachers do to be responsive, instead of directive, during an interaction? We need to create a culture in the classroom in which students' verbal contributions are valued. To do this, we need to respond to every contribution in a way that shows we care about what students say. We can do this by responding to the student's topic, answering the student's questions, and helping the student say more on that same topic. As a general rule, we want to use more comments than questions; but when we do use questions we want them to be genuine (rather than test questions), to be open-ended, to continue the student's topic, or to clarify the student's talk by eliciting missing information. Responsive interactions are not too fast or too slow; they follow a pace that helps students feel comfortable talking.

Read the following excerpt of a teacher introducing a new book to three students. Note the directive style and think about how the interaction might have been more responsive toward students.

Teacher: Who can tell me what you think this book is about?
Mimi: Cats.
Teacher: Raise your hand.
Mimi: (Raises her hand)
Teacher: Okay, Mimi.
Mimi: Cats.
Teacher: Who can tell me something about a cat?
Edgar: I have a cat.
Teacher: I'll tell you something I know; cats have whiskers.

Did you notice that the teacher is concerned about controlling the students' hand-raising behavior? This is particularly interesting because this teacher is reading to only three students rather than the whole class. When she asks students to tell her something about a cat, one student mentions that he has a cat, but the teacher was expecting some characteristics of cats. Therefore, when the student's response does not fit that agenda, she offers a model. While modeling is one way of showing students what she is expecting, the directiveness of the interaction signals to the students that their responses need to match her expectations (there is a right answer here). Also, to respond, they must do so in a rigid fashion (by raising their hand). By the end of this read aloud, all three students were disengaged, reluctant to offer any answers to her repeated wh-questions, and focused more on the fuzz on the carpet squares than the book.

Imagine what might have happened if the teacher had been responsive rather than directive.

> *Teacher:* Who can tell me what you think this book is about?
> *Mimi:* Cats.
> *Teacher:* Why do you think this book is about cats?
> *Mimi:* Because I saw a picture of a cat on the front.
> *Teacher:* Okay; you used a picture clue. Great strategy. So, who can tell me something about a cat?
> *Edgar:* I have a cat.
> *Teacher:* You have a cat at home? Wow, tell me something about your cat.
> *Edgar:* My cat's name is Waldo.
> *Teacher:* Oh, that's a great name. Tell me something about what Waldo looks like.
> *Edgar:* He orange.
> *Teacher:* He's orange. So Waldo has orange fur. You're telling me what your cat looks like. Someone else tell me some parts a cat has on its body.
> *Mimi:* Eyes.
> *Edgar:* Claws.
> *Teacher:* So cats have eyes on their face like we do. And they have claws. Do we have claws?
> *Students:* No!!
> *Crystal:* But we got this part here (pointing to her fingernails).
> *Teacher:* You're right; we have fingernails but not claws.
> *Crystal:* Got a nose with things sticking out.
> *Teacher:* (Waits—and points to the whiskers in the illustration)
> *Edgar:* Those are um . . . um . . . whiskers.
> *Mimi:* On his face . . . like um hairs.
> *Teacher:* Oh, so cats have a nose with whiskers sticking out around his nose. Well, this book tells us what they do with those whiskers and about other parts a cat has on its body, so let's listen and learn what parts a cat has.

In this example, the topic was maintained for multiple turns with a number of different students participating in the interaction. The teacher accepts the student responses and builds on them. The responsive style encourages more students to participate, and the students feel comfortable doing so.

When adults are highly directive, asking questions or issuing commands with a specific response in mind, it restricts how students can respond, and this makes it more likely that students will fail or withdraw from the interaction. It also results in short answers with simple grammar rather than longer sentences that convey complex ideas. Therefore, we should strive to be responsive, and to balance the number of turns we take as opposed to dominating the interaction. Students will have greater motivation to participate, and their contributions likely will be more complex both in terms of the ideas they contain and the grammar they use. See Figure 2.1 for a list of characteristics of a responsive style of interaction contrasted with a directive style.

Figure 2.1. Features of a Responsive Style of Interaction Contrasted with a Directive Style of Interaction

Responsive Style of Interaction	Directive Style of Interaction
Use more comments than questions	Ask the students many questions
Answer the student's questions	Answer the student's questions
Follow the student's topic (i.e., be contingent) or guide back to the topic at hand	Direct the topics of conversation (i.e., push our own agenda)
Allow plenty of wait time for a response	Allow minimum wait time for a response
Keep an appropriate pace—use cues from the students to judge the pacing of the conversation (both how much wait time to allow for each student and how quickly you follow up on what the student says)	Keep the pace of the interactions moving quickly
Balance the interaction—the student and teacher talk about the same amount or the students talk more than the teacher	Dominate the interaction—the teacher talks more than students
Ask questions that are primarily • Genuine—we don't already know the answer; they are not "test questions" • Open-ended—there are many possible responses • Topic-continuing—they continue the topic of discussion or a topic a student introduces • Clarifying—they elicit missing information that can clarify the child's intended meaning	Ask questions that are primarily • Test questions—there is a right or wrong answer; the teacher verifies or provides the right answer • Closed-ended—there is one appropriate answer • Topic-changing—they change the topic a student introduces • Directive—they demand specific information

SUMMARY

In this chapter, we highlighted the importance of responding to students' talk in ways that create an environment conducive for rich discussions. To achieve this, we explored ways that teachers can use a responsive style during various classroom activities. Mastering the art of a responsive interaction style establishes a foundation that can then be applied during read alouds to achieve high-quality instructional interactions.

CHAPTER 3

Responsive Scaffolding Strategies for an Interactive Read Aloud

When teachers use a responsive style of interacting in the classroom, and specifically during read alouds, students start to talk . . . a lot! These discussions create opportunities to provide scaffolding that can help students advance their speaking abilities, their comprehension, and the depth of their knowledge in a discipline. Teachers can capitalize on these opportunities, all within an engaging and fun interaction around a book.

At the same time, however, lots of talk can be challenging to manage. Students' comments and questions might reveal limited language abilities with sentences that are poorly formulated or hard to interpret. They may reveal misunderstandings about the content or vocabulary. Some students' contributions may be tangential to the topic. In all cases, we have the opportunity to support the students' language and build their knowledge. On the other hand, some students' comments might reveal a deep and perceptive connection to content from another text or from their own lives. They might reveal reasoning and insights that provide an opportunity to extend the discussion. Whether a student's verbal contribution falls short of the expectation or is surprisingly astute, it provides a window into what the student needs in order to learn more. As teachers, we have the opportunity to help students move forward with their learning. We can do this by providing a scaffold that is tailored to each student's particular need.

WHAT IS SCAFFOLDING?

Scaffolding is the support we provide to students to help them achieve more than they are capable of on their own. We gradually withdraw that support as the student is able to do the task independently. The idea of scaffolding comes from social learning theories (Bruner, 1986; Vygotsky, 1962), which view the interaction between a student and a more competent person as foundational for learning. Scaffolding can be challenging, however, because it requires that we make two forms of judgments about our students' abilities:

1. When planning for a read aloud, teachers must judge students'
   current abilities and background knowledge and decide what to teach,
   how to structure our time, and what types of questions to ask.
2. During a read aloud, teachers must judge the content and language in
   a student's contribution in order to determine what type of scaffolding
   will be most effective in that moment.

The first judgment is done in the planning of the read aloud. The second,
however, must be done quickly and with little time to analyze the situation.
Providing too much support limits a student's opportunity to learn, while providing too little support can result in failure on the task, a decrease in the
student's motivation, and reluctance to take risks in the future. Therefore, it is
important to provide the right amount of support.

The Gradual Release of Responsibility Model by Pearson and Gallagher
(1983) illustrates how adult and student roles in any task change over the
course of time (see Figure 3.1). During an instructional activity, the student
and teacher (or more competent peer) work together. When a student is first
learning something in the classroom (left side of the diagram), the teacher
typically takes on the majority of the control and provides a high amount

Figure 3.1. Gradual Release of Responsibility Model

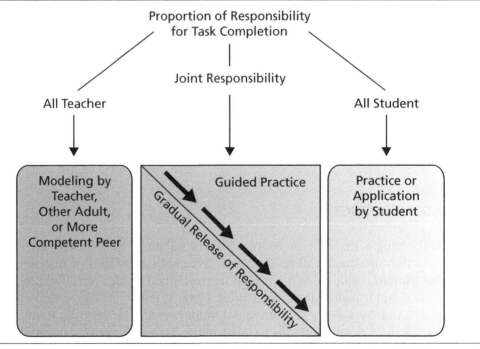

From Pearson, D., & Gallagher, M. (1983). The instruction of reading comprehension. *Contemporary Educational Psychology, 8*(3), 317–344.

of support for the student. Thus, the teacher's role in the task is substantial, while the student's role is minimal. As the student is able, he or she takes on more responsibility for completing the task, and the teacher decreases support (moving from the left to the right side of diagram). Hence, the student's role in the task becomes greater and greater, and at the same time, the teacher's role in the task becomes less and less. Our job as teachers is to determine where the student is on the continuum at any given moment and to respond by providing the appropriate type and amount of support.

THREE TYPES OF SCAFFOLDING STRATEGIES TEACHERS CAN PROVIDE

How does scaffolding work during a read aloud? Teachers listen to a student's verbal contribution and evaluate its content and language. Then teachers match their scaffolding to the needs of that student. Our system of scaffolding includes three options at any given moment during a read aloud. Teachers can provide

1. High-Support Strategies
2. Low-Support Strategies
3. Raise-the-Bar Strategies

When using ***High-Support Strategies***, a teacher takes on most of the responsibility for the joint task by modeling, explaining, and eliciting responses. That is, the teacher stays to the left side of the diagram in Figure 3.1, providing maximum support to the student. We use High-Support scaffolding when we know students have limited knowledge and we need to provide High Support right from the start. Alternatively, we use High-Support Strategies when we want to give students an opportunity to participate easily and successfully, or we want students to learn to verbally display their knowledge. Finally, we use High-Support Strategies when a student's contribution reveals major confusion about the content or language that is weak.

When using ***Low-Support Strategies***, a teacher provides some support for a student but begins to expect him or her to take on more responsibility for the task. In this case, the teacher and student jointly construct meaning and have shared roles in the task. This is illustrated in the middle of the diagram in Figure 3.1. We use Low-Support Scaffolding when we believe our students have the ability to improve their contribution with a little help from us. We choose it when a student exhibits minor confusions about the content or the student's language is ambiguous and we need more information in order to proceed.

When using ***Raise-the-Bar Strategies***, the teacher minimizes his or her role and increases the demand on the student to achieve greater depth of knowledge, more sophisticated thinking, or more complex language. This is illustrated at the right side of the diagram in Figure 3.1. We use Raise-the-Bar

Strategies in order to provide opportunities for students to reach higher levels of cognitive thinking. Thus, we plan questions ahead of time that will require students to predict, infer, make connections, compare/contrast, consider points of view or the author's craft, define words, or explain text features. All students need such opportunities, even students with learning differences. In fact, students with learning differences often get fewer opportunities to respond to questions at higher levels of cognitive thinking, and that further exacerbates the gap between their abilities and those of peers who are typically developing. Students with learning differences need both opportunities to talk at this level and scaffolding from us to help them craft their responses. Another time to use Raise-the-Bar Strategies is during a read aloud when a student's contribution shows good understanding of the content with language that is clear and relatively grammatically correct. We ask them Raise the Bar questions to push them even further in their thinking.

Let's discuss the options we have within each of these three types of strategies and when to use each type. All of the strategies are shown in the flowchart in Figure 3.2. In addition, Figure 3.3 on pp. 30–31 outlines Raise-the-Bar Strategies for three genres: literature, informational texts, and poetry.

HIGH-SUPPORT STRATEGIES

The purpose of High-Support Strategies is to make the task easier for a student and to ensure a high degree of success. The teacher provides a high amount of support, leaving little room for error as the student responds. High-Support Strategies are useful for all students, but they are especially important for students who are ELLs or students with disabilities. Although as teachers we may believe we are providing sufficient High-Support scaffolding, there is some evidence that we may be failing to support some students adequately during the read aloud (Pentimonti & Justice, 2010). High-Support Strategies are good options in the following circumstances:

- When a student has limited knowledge or skill
- When we want a student to have quick success
- When we want to boost a student's confidence
- When a student is reticent or fearful of taking risks. Any student may become reticent for some reason; however, this may be more typical of ELLs and students with learning differences

High-Support Strategies include

1. Modeling, defining, and explaining
2. Asking supportive, closed-ended questions to increase success

Figure 3.2. Flowchart for Selecting Scaffolding Strategies

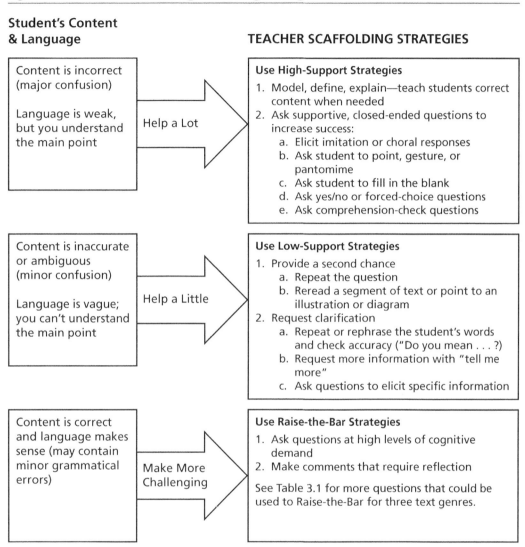

Student's Content & Language

TEACHER SCAFFOLDING STRATEGIES

Content is incorrect (major confusion)

Language is weak, but you understand the main point

Help a Lot

Use High-Support Strategies

1. Model, define, explain—teach students correct content when needed
2. Ask supportive, closed-ended questions to increase success:
   a. Elicit imitation or choral responses
   b. Ask student to point, gesture, or pantomime
   c. Ask student to fill in the blank
   d. Ask yes/no or forced-choice questions
   e. Ask comprehension-check questions

Content is inaccurate or ambiguous (minor confusion)

Language is vague; you can't understand the main point

Help a Little

Use Low-Support Strategies

1. Provide a second chance
   a. Repeat the question
   b. Reread a segment of text or point to an illustration or diagram
2. Request clarification
   a. Repeat or rephrase the student's words and check accuracy ("Do you mean . . . ?)
   b. Request more information with "tell me more"
   c. Ask questions to elicit specific information

Content is correct and language makes sense (may contain minor grammatical errors)

Make More Challenging

Use Raise-the-Bar Strategies

1. Ask questions at high levels of cognitive demand
2. Make comments that require reflection

See Table 3.1 for more questions that could be used to Raise-the-Bar for three text genres.

Model, Define, and Explain

At times it is clear that the students do not understand our questions or they are confused about the content of a text. Thus, they might produce several responses that are clearly off the mark. In that case, we need to give the students correct information quickly and decisively. If we do not, we risk students' inadvertently retaining the incorrect information, and it can be hard to correct their confusion later. Therefore, after we get several wrong answers, it is better to stop eliciting more responses from students and instead give them the correct information. In this case, we need to model our thinking, define

text continues on p. 32

Figure 3.3. Raise-the-Bar Strategies for Each Genre of Text

Task	Literature	Informational Texts	Poetry
Inferences/ Predictions	Make inferences that are not explicitly stated in the text Predict what will happen next in a story Make inferences about a character's feelings	Make inferences that are not explicitly stated in the text Make inferences about photographs, diagrams, maps, or charts	Make inferences that are not explicitly stated in the text, including those about the topic or mood of the poem
Experiential connections	Relate the story to one's own life experiences	Identify how the information in the text applies to one's own life	Relate the poem to one's own life experiences
Compare/ Contrast within text	Identify similarities and differences among characters	Identify similarities and differences related to the topic (e.g., animals, people/cultures)	Compare and contrast subject matter within the text or descriptive language (adjectives) within a poem
Compare/ Contrast across texts	Compare and contrast stories or different versions of the same story	Compare and contrast information given in two different texts on the same topic	Compare and contrast two poems with the same theme
Explain ideas or thinking & use text or illustrations as evidence	Explain thoughts and ideas about the story Use illustrations or text to explain or support thinking	Explain information/ideas from the text Use graphics, illustrations, or text to clarify or provide evidence	Explain thinking about the poem Use illustrations or text to support thinking
Points of view	Identify characters' points of view and provide evidence from the story Identify the narrator's point of view (1st person, 2nd person, 3rd person)	Identify author's point of view Evaluate the information provided in relation to other sources	Identify author's point of view and provide evidence from the poem

Define words	Define words, especially for more sophisticated vocabulary Provide evidence from the text or other sources for the meaning of a word	Define words, especially for technical vocabulary on the topic Provide evidence from the text for the meaning of a word	Define words or phrases, including made-up words or words used in novel ways Provide evidence from the text or other sources for the meaning of a word Compare meanings of two similar words
Explain text features or structures	Discuss features of the narrative structure (e.g., characters, setting, goals, resolution) Explain how characters develop over time given their goals and challenges	Identify the main topic versus key details from the text Explain text features that help the student locate information	Identify how the author's choices regarding font, spacing, or other text features contribute to the poem
Author's craft	Explain why the author chose one word/phrase over another word/phrase Describe why the author chose the events in the story Describe the lesson or moral the author wants to convey Describe the feelings the author wants to invoke	Identify the author's main purpose and describe what the author wants the reader to learn	Explain why the author chose one word/phrase over another word/phrase Describe the message the author wants to convey Describe the feelings the author wants to invoke
Explain how words convey mood, tone, or feelings	Describe how words/phrases affect the mood or add meaning to the story	Describe how the words in the text make the information convincing	Describe how words/phrases affect the tone or mood of the poem Describe how words and phrases appeal to the senses, or how they support rhythm

words, and explain concepts. We could also choose to use visuals to help support their comprehension, such as illustrations, objects, models, diagrams,
charts, or graphs. Such visuals might be available in the book we are reading
aloud, or we might need to find other sources for visuals and bring them into
the instructional moment.

There are three strategies teachers could use with this type of scaffold.

A. *Model your own thinking.* Modeling our own thinking illustrates the
kind of reasoning we are doing while reading the text. For example:

> *Teacher:* See that boxer (dog) prickin' his ears up? He's trying to listen
> to something far away. (Modeling an inference made from the
> illustration)

B. *Give a definition.* Giving a definition allows us to teach vocabulary
that is important for comprehension of the text. When students are confused,
it may be because they do not understand a word being used in the text.
Defining a word for them can help to clear up the confusion. For example:

> *Student:* Huge wings! (Noticing the diagram of a bat)
> *Teacher:* Yeah, that's called its wingspan. A wingspan means when the bat
> has his wings open wide like this (gesture), that's called a wingspan.
> We can measure it from the tip here to the tip over here to see how
> long it is.

C. *Explain a concept.* Explaining a concept allows us to teach exactly what
the students need to know in order to comprehend the text. We may need to
provide some piece of background knowledge or explain a new idea presented
in the text with more clarity using visuals to aid comprehension. In the following example, the teacher is reading *Moondance* (Asch, 1993), about Little
Bear, who is jumping into a puddle and dancing with the moon. The text does
not state that the bear is dancing with the *reflection* of the moon he sees in the
puddle. Therefore, the teacher chooses to explain it.

> *Teacher:* So we don't just use a mirror for a reflection. Sometimes we can
> see the reflection in water as well. That's what the bear was seeing.
> He was seeing a reflection of the moon in the water and it seemed like
> the moon had really come down to dance with him!

Ask Supportive, Closed-Ended Questions to Increase Success

Another way to provide High-Support Scaffolding is to ask questions that limit what is required by the student, in terms of both content and language,

because the goal is for the student to be able to produce an accurate response. Such High Support minimizes students' errors in content or language. In order to achieve this, we can use the following five strategies.

A. Elicit an imitation or choral response. We can model the information a student needs and then elicit an imitation from an individual student or a choral response from the class. This strategy also has been called co-participating (Pentimonti & Justice, 2010). Eliciting an imitation works well when we want to give students practice with new words or information. When we elicit an imitation, it engages students actively and they are more likely to retain the word or information. For example:

> *Teacher: Snout*; everybody say that word.
> *Students:* Snout.
> *Teacher:* That's right.

B. Ask the student to point, gesture, or pantomime. We can also create a High-Support Scaffold by asking a student to point, to gesture, or to act out a response rather than use words and sentences. This significantly reduces the demands on a student's expressive language but still allows active participation. Allowing pointing, gesturing, or acting out can be helpful for our students with disabilities or those who are ELLs. For example, this teacher had all students participate nonverbally:

> *Teacher: Ferocious*; that means he looked really mean and scary. Show me a ferocious face.

C. Ask the student to fill in the blank. A fill-in-the-blank request is another way to reduce what students are required to do. We can make a statement but leave off the last word or several words so students will fill them in. To do this, we slow down before the missing words and use intonation to signal to students to finish the statement. Fill-in-the-blank requests are High Support because we provide the majority of the sentence and students need to generate only a few words. These have also been called "cloze procedures." For example:

> *Teacher:* When hot, why does a pig get in the mud?
> *Student:* So they won't get sick.
> *Teacher:* That's right. They need to keep their skin _____.
> *Student:* Moist.
> *Teacher:* If a pig's skin doesn't stay moist it gets _____.
> *Student:* Sick.
> *Teacher:* It gets sick, that's right.

D. Ask yes/no and forced-choice questions. Yes/no questions are inherently supportive and the language required is minimal. In addition, the question itself contains supportive information. We can provide greater support by pointing to the illustrations, adding a gesture, or using intonation cues that signal the correct response. Likewise, with a forced choice, we provide two answers and ask the student to select one answer. A forced choice provides a model for the language or content that the student needs in order to respond. We could provide two equally good options, or we could provide a choice between a wrong answer and a right answer. If one of the two options is a better choice, we can add an intonation cue to signal to the student the best answer. Adding the intonation cue provides even higher support. In the following example the teacher asked a forced-choice question with intonation support:

> *Teacher:* Do you think the moon is always out there or do you think it disappears during the day?
> *Student:* It disappears at night.
> *Teacher:* It disappears at night, or *appears* at night? (Forced-choice question with intonation cue on *appears*)
> *Student:* Appears.
> *Teacher:* It *appears* at night.

In another example, this teacher started with a forced-choice question and then followed up with a yes/no question and then a fill-in-the-blank question:

> *Teacher:* So what is it now? Daytime or nighttime? (Forced-choice question)
> *Students:* (Some students say "daytime," some say "nighttime")
> *Teacher:* Is it nighttime out there? (Yes/no question with a skeptical intonation)
> *Student:* No.
> *Student:* It's cloudy.
> *Teacher:* It's cloudy, but it's day . . . _____. (Fill-in-the-blank question)
> *Student:* Time!
> *Teacher:* Daytime, yes.

E. Ask comprehension-check questions. Comprehension checks are questions that are closed-ended with a known answer. We use them to elicit background knowledge or specific information that students should be able to remember from the text. Comprehension checks also give students a chance to verbally display knowledge. They can give students quick success, which bolsters their confidence. They can also reveal what students are confused about. In the following example, the teacher is interested in knowing what students recall about how to help protect bats:

> *Teacher:* So what could we do to make sure bats are safe? (Showing the illustrations and the text that just told ways to protect bats)
> *Student:* Make the houses.
> *Teacher:* We should make them some houses. What else?
> *Student:* Um, take them to the place we went . . . um, I forgot.
> *Teacher:* Take them to Prairie Park Nature Center? Yeah.

LOW-SUPPORT STRATEGIES

The purpose of Low-Support Strategies is to encourage students to take on more of the responsibility for the task, while still providing a little help. Low-Support Strategies are useful when students have some familiarity with and ability to discuss the topic or concepts in the text, but they might need some support to fully comprehend or express their ideas. We use Low-Support Strategies when we believe a student is capable of a better response in that moment and we also believe the student can tolerate making corrections in front of his or her peers. If the student will find it too embarrassing to make corrections in front of the class, then it is best to provide High Support instead. Low-Support Strategies include

1. Providing a second chance
2. Requesting clarification

Provide a Second Chance

The first approach to providing Low Support is to give the student a second chance to share the idea. The student can alter the content or the language to improve the contribution, rather than the teacher taking over and providing High Support. There are two ways to provide a second chance.

A. Repeat the question. Repeating the question serves two purposes. First, it serves to focus the student's attention on the content of the question, perhaps with intonation to highlight certain words. Second, it signals that the student's contribution is insufficient and gives the student an opportunity to try again. For example, this teacher asks her question again in a slightly different way and gets a correct answer:

> *Teacher:* The tail begins to disappear and what happens [to the tadpole]?
> *Student:* They turn into frogs.
> *Teacher:* What happens when the tail disappears?
> *Student:* They grow feet.
> *Teacher:* They grow their feet and then they turn into frogs.

B. Reread a segment of text or point to an illustration or diagram. Rereading the text signals to students that something is incorrect about their response, and it gives them the opportunity to listen again to the text. After we reread text that contains the information needed to generate a correct response, the student is responsible for generating her or his own response from scratch. Therefore, rereading text provides Low Support. Similarly, we can provide Low Support by pointing to an illustration, diagram, or other visual that helps the student correct the error. This signals a need to modify the contribution and that the visual support provides information that can help the student do that more successfully. For example:

> *Teacher:* So do pigs want to be clean or dirty?
> *Student:* Dirty.
> *Teacher:* Listen again to what it says in the text. Listen. (Teacher rereads text explaining that pigs are tidy animals that prefer to be clean)
> *Teacher:* Do they want to be clean or dirty? (Repeats original question)
> *Student:* Clean.
> *Teacher:* They want to be clean. The text says pigs like to be clean all the time. Interesting; I didn't know that.

Request Clarification

The second way to provide Low Support is to request clarification from a student. Requesting clarification gives us a chance to better understand what the student means, and it gives the student a chance to formulate a better response. Upon clarification, it may become apparent that the student is more confused than we thought, in which case we might move on to High Support instead! Or the student might add to his or her response, demonstrating correct information and better language use, and we could move on to Raising the Bar. In any case, requesting clarification gives us a bit more time and information to determine what the student needs most. We can request clarification in three ways.

A. Repeat or rephrase the student's words and check accuracy. When a student's contribution to a discussion exhibits either errors in language use or errors in content, it can be helpful to rephrase what the student said and ask if we got it right. Sometimes a student's grammar makes it difficult to fully understand what he or she is trying to convey. Rephrasing the sentence provides a model of the appropriate language but, more important, allows us to determine if we understood what the student meant. It's important to fully understand the student's contribution in order to choose the best scaffolding strategy. In the following example, a teacher checks to see if students understand what is happening to the two ants in Van Allsburg's (1988) *Two Bad Ants.*

Teacher: So what is happening to the ants? What does a "shower of crystals" and "a boiling brown lake" mean?

Student: They're falling sugar and coffee.

Teacher: The ants are falling into the coffee with the sugar?

Student: Yeah.

B. Request more information with "tell me more." Students often give us a partial response rather than one that is fully developed. Therefore, asking them to "tell me more" gives the student an opportunity to add to their contribution or reformulate the idea. A "tell me more" prompt may be all that is needed for them to generate a full and accurate response; however, if it is not, their additions help us decide how to tailor our scaffolding. In the following example, the teacher starts with a Raise the Bar question about narrative text features:

Teacher: Today we're going to start talking about characters. Does anyone have an idea about what characters are?

Logan: In a movie.

Teacher: Something in a movie. Tell me more.

Logan: King Kong.

Teacher: Okay; I think you have it in your head. I'm going to ask someone else to see if she can help explain it a little bit more. Isabella?

Isabella: People in a movie. They would be characters.

Teacher: So the people in a movie are characters? I would agree with that. So, how does that work with our reading? We're talking about reading right now, so what is a character when we're reading? (Back to the original question)

Amelia: Little Red Riding Hood or her mom.

Teacher: Okay; can you explain that a little bit more? (Basically a "tell me more" prompt)

Amelia: No.

Teacher: No. Logan, can you help her out? Amelia said like Little Red Riding Hood or her mom are characters, so can we figure out a definition of what a character is? (Back to the original question)

Logan: It's a person that is in the book.

Teacher: Right. The people or sometimes animals in stories are the characters and they do something in the story. They speak or they do an action.

C. Ask questions to elicit specific information. We can also provide Low Support by asking specific questions to elicit information that will help the student clarify his or her contribution. These can be open-ended questions, such as "Why do you think that happened?" or "How did you come to that conclusion?" Questions also could be closed-ended to elicit specific information. Such Low Support questions help the students verbalize information or ideas that they can then use to create a more elaborate response to our original question. After the student provides clarification, we often repeat our original question to give them another chance to answer.

In summary, when we provide Low-Support Strategies, a student has an opportunity to revise and add to the original response. If the student's new contribution makes sense, we can accept it and move on, or we might choose to raise the bar to push the student even further. Alternatively, if the student's second or third attempt continues to show errors in content or language, we can switch to High-Support Strategies.

RAISE-THE-BAR STRATEGIES

The purpose of Raise-the-Bar Strategies is to help students achieve higher levels of cognitive thinking, more complex language expression, and a deeper understanding of the text. Raise-the-Bar Strategies are useful when students are already familiar with the topic, concepts, and vocabulary in the text or have had previous exposure to it (e.g., on a second or third repeated reading of the text). When a student contribution contains accurate content with good language formulation (i.e., no errors or only minor grammatical errors), we can help the student and the class by taking the discussion to a greater depth of understanding. Raising the Bar is one way to differentiate instruction for students who are ready for this challenge.

Teachers might be worried that Raise-the-Bar Strategies would be too challenging for some students in the class. That may be true. However, all students in the group do *not* have to be at this higher level in order for teachers to engage some students at a higher level of cognitive thinking. It is important to challenge the students who are ready for that, not to hold them back because others in the class might not understand the discussion. And students benefit from hearing those discussions even when they cannot fully participate in them yet. Consequently, it is important to *plan* ahead for ways to raise the bar during a read aloud. In the planning for a read aloud, teachers can consider the genre of text and choose several ways to raise the bar that match the learning objectives for the read aloud. Figure 3.3 includes specific ways to raise the bar that are appropriate for the genre of text. These methods of raising the bar will be defined and discussed in the chapters that follow on each genre of text.

CHOOSING THE APPROPRIATE SCAFFOLDING STRATEGY

While we are conducting the read aloud, we must choose what scaffolding strategies to use in the moment after a student says something. The flowchart in Figure 3.2 shows each of the types of strategies and when to use them during a read aloud. Undeniably, choosing strategies during the read aloud is challenging because we must think on our feet and respond within a matter of seconds! One way of matching support strategies to the student in the moment is to ask ourselves the following:

Do I want to help the student a lot? —> Then provide High Support
Do I want to help the student a little? —> Then provide Low Support
Do I want to make it more challenging for the student? —> Then
    provide Raise-the-Bar Support

In short, we think to ourselves, "Help a lot? Help a little? Make it more challenging?" This thinking has helped us to improve our own ability to choose the right level of support in the moment. We can also improve our ability to choose the right scaffolding strategy by planning ahead for the interactions. Planning depends on the genre of text being read during the read aloud, and that is the focus of the chapters on reading aloud literature (Chapter 5), informational texts (Chapter 6), poetry (Chapter 7). and digital texts (Chapter 8).

SUMMARY

In this chapter, we considered how to provide responsive scaffolding to students during read alouds so that students get just the right amount of support at just the right time. To do this, we describe specific strategies to help students a lot (High Support), strategies to help students a little (Low Support), and strategies to make it more challenging (Raise the Bar). In addition, we considered how to choose the right level of scaffolding in the moment during the read aloud.

CHAPTER 4

Using the Responsive-Interactive Scaffolding Strategies to Support Learning

Reading aloud provides many opportunities for teachers and students to engage in discussions that involve multiple students and multiple turns. Indeed, the goal is to get everyone talking about the story, informational text, or poem! But all that talk makes our role during the read aloud even more challenging. As soon as a student offers a verbal contribution, we are on the spot to decide what to do or say next in order to support that student in the best way and to keep the discussion on track to fulfill our learning objectives. We want to provide the right kind of scaffolding, in the right amount, at the right time. So, should we provide High Support to reduce cognitive and language demands placed on the student? Should we provide Low Support so students can clarify or improve upon their contribution? Should we raise the bar by asking questions that require high levels of cognitive thinking? We have only seconds to decide! Although highly skilled teachers make it look easy, it rarely is; it requires thoughtfulness every time we respond. But it is also true that we can improve our skill at providing responsive-interactive scaffolding through practice and reflection.

In this chapter, we show teachers in action, applying the strategies and helping students do more than they would be capable of independently. Also, as you will see, these teachers often use a variety of strategies during an interaction. They move from Raise the Bar to Low Support to High Support as needed when responding to students' verbal contributions in order to scaffold learning.

EXAMPLES OF HIGH-SUPPORT STRATEGIES

High-Support Strategies are useful because they provide full support and ensure success. We might choose to use High-Support Strategies in order to

- Teach or provide background knowledge up front
- Dispel confusion or support weak language
- Check comprehension or elicit a verbal display of knowledge

Teach or Provide Background Knowledge

Sometimes we begin a read aloud with High-Support Strategies because we want to be sure our students have the background information they need to understand the content. We model, explain, or define. For example, during the reading of *Tale of a Tadpole* (Wallace, 1998), the learning objective was to teach informational text features. The teacher chose to use High Support because students did not have much prior knowledge of informational text features.

> *Teacher:* See that little picture there? It's showing us a close-up of the frog's webbed toes. The author wants us to be able to see the details of the webbing in between each of the toes. So she used this little picture with a label so we could learn what it is called (pointing to label) "webbed toes." See on our list of text features? (pointing to the Text Features Anchor Chart) These are called "pictures with captions or labels." This is something authors use in this kind of book—a book that teaches us about a topic.

Dispel Confusion or Support Weak Language

Sometimes we need to use High Support in order to dispel confusion or support a student whose language was weak. In this example, although the teacher started by asking a Raise the Bar question, she then used both Low Support and High Support in order to correct a misunderstanding about the content:

> *Teacher:* What does *migrate* mean, Dustin? (Raise the Bar: define word)
> *Dustin:* Um, migrate.
> *Teacher:* When birds migrate. In winter. What does that mean? (Low Support: request clarification)
> *Dustin:* Sleep.
> *Teacher:* Is that migrate or is that hibernation? (High Support: forced-choice question)
> *Dustin:* Hibernation.
> *Teacher:* It's hibernation. Kristy, what does *migrate* mean? (Raise the Bar: define word)
> *Kristy: Migrate* means the birds go south so they can be warm.

Teacher: Excellent; they go south in the winter so they can be warm. Bats do the same thing. They migrate to a different place where they can be warm.

Check Comprehension or Elicit a Verbal Display of Knowledge

Finally, another reason for using High Support is to check students' comprehension or to ask students to verbally display their knowledge. For example, this teacher is using High Support to check students' background knowledge before reading the poem "Fog" by Carl Sandburg.

Teacher: Do you know what fog is? (High Support: comprehension check)
Elizabeth: Yes, yes, yes! It's like mist.
Teacher: It is like mist.
Maria: It's like a bunch of gray clouds falling from the sky. My daddy told me that and I thought like it was gray clouds falling out of bed.
Serena: It's like foggy and you can't see anything.
Teacher: So you all said it's like mist and gray clouds falling out of bed and you really can't see anything when it's foggy outside. Now we're going to listen to the poem "Fog" by Carl Sandburg, and I want you to think about how he describes fog.

Asking students to tell us what they know about a topic is not only a good way to informally assess their knowledge or learning; it also helps students to activate their background knowledge about that topic and prepares them for the read aloud. In sum, we can use High-Support Strategies to ensure that students are learning basic information presented in the text, which will be needed to understand more complex concepts presented later.

EXAMPLES OF LOW-SUPPORT STRATEGIES

Although High Support helps to ensure student success, we also need to encourage students to move toward independence. Our goal is to *gradually* release responsibility. Low-Support Strategies are the answer. We move from High Support, where we are responsible for most of the task, to Low Support, where the student participates jointly with us in the task. Low-Support Strategies provide students the opportunity to do more on their own. Depending on how the student responds to Low-Support Strategies, teachers need to be ready to switch to High Support or to Raise-the-Bar Support. Let's look at some examples.

Rephrasing and Requesting More Information

During a read aloud, there are times when students' contributions are ambiguous. Either they are fuzzy on the details regarding content or their language is vague, but the result is that we just can't be sure what they mean. In those cases, offering High Support right away doesn't work well. For one, High Support might be unnecessary; the student might be able to produce a more clear response on her or his own. In addition, it can be hard to figure out exactly what High Support to provide. We may not know enough about what the student is trying to say; therefore, our High Support could be way off the mark! In these cases, we can ask students to clarify their contribution, or we can ask questions that help them add more to their idea.

In this example, the teacher has finished reading *The Magic Fish* (Littledale & Pels, 1985). She begins the discussion with Raise the Bar questions requiring a student to make an inference about a character's feeling and then to provide evidence for her reasoning. The student provides a response that is somewhat confusing, so the teacher rephrases the student's response to be sure she understood it.

> *Teacher:* How do you think the fisherman feels at the end of the story? Denise? (Raise the Bar: inference)
>
> *Denise:* Happy.
>
> *Teacher:* Why do you say that? (Raise the Bar: explain idea, provide evidence)
>
> *Denise:* 'Cause in the first one he was happy and then his wife said, "Go and get me more." But now he's back in this one (points to picture) and he's happy.
>
> *Teacher:* Hmm, I'll tell you what I think you're saying and you tell me if I'm right, okay? I think you're saying the fisherman was happy when he lived in this house (points). Then his wife made him unhappy with all her wishes and changes to the house but now the fisherman is back here in this first house (points) and he's happy again. Is that what you're saying? (Low Support: rephrase student's words to check accuracy)
>
> *Denise:* Yeah, he's happy because he's back in his first house.

In another example, the teacher read a poem called "The Rain" (in Prelutsky & Brown, 1986). A student uses an unusual word choice and the teacher requests clarification.

> *Teacher:* The poet told us what she thinks about when it rains; what do you think about when it rains? (Raise the Bar: personal connection)

Jack: I think about my shield and the rain goes "ting, ting . . . ting, ting."
Teacher: A shield? Why do you think about a shield in the rain? (Low Support: request clarification)
Jack: So my hair can't get wet. I hold it like this (gestures holding a shield over his head) and I don't get wet when I hold a shield over my head.

Asking a Low Support question or requesting, "Tell me more," gives the student a chance to reformulate the idea or add more to it. The additional information helps us better respond to the student and also provides the chance to jointly construct meaning.

Reread a Section of the Text

Finally, rather than simply giving a student information (High Support: model, define, explain) or asking more questions (Low Support: request clarification), we can provide support by encouraging students to listen to the text again as we reread it. For example, the teacher in the following example tells her students that she will be reading a simple book, *Mrs. Wishy Washy* (Cowley, 1999). After reading, she wants students to describe how Mrs. Wishy Washy is feeling and provide evidence from the text or illustrations. The teacher reads the story without interruption.

Teacher: All right; now that we read the story, I'm going to go back and read it again and if you think you know how Mrs. Wishy Washy is feeling, I want you to raise your hand. (Begins rereading the text)
Teacher: Oh, a lot of us think we know how Mrs. Wishy Washy feels. How do you think Mrs. Wishy Washy feels, Christian? (Raise the Bar: inference)
Christian: Surprised.
Teacher: Surprised? Tell me more. (Low Support: request more information)
Christian: She screamed.
Teacher: Hmm. You could scream when you're surprised but let's think about the story. What do you think she feels mostly? She said, "Just look at you!" (Low Support: Rereads text in a very loud voice)
Christian: Mad.
Teacher: What kind of voice was I using? (High Support: comprehension check)
Christian: A loud voice.
Teacher: So how did Mrs. Wishy Washy feel and how do you know? (Repeats original question; Raise the Bar: inference)
Christian: She's mad and I know because she's screaming.

Providing Low Support for students gives them the opportunity to jointly construct meaning. We are gradually releasing responsibility for the task, encouraging them to do more and backing off on the support we provide. In this way, Low Support becomes a tool for helping students achieve more independence, while still providing enough scaffolding for them to be successful.

EXAMPLES OF RAISE-THE-BAR STRATEGIES

Raise-the-Bar Strategies are intended to give students opportunities to talk at high levels of cognitive thinking. We often plan Raise the Bar questions to ask during or after a read aloud to elicit inferring, predicting, making connections, comparing, contrasting, explaining, considering points of view, and defining words or describing how they convey mood or tone. Although most of these can be achieved during read alouds of any genre, different genres provide different opportunities to raise the bar. Let's look at a few examples of ways we might raise the bar in the context of three genres—literature, informational texts, and poetry.

Literature

Literature provides unique opportunities to make inferences and predictions, relate a story to our own lives, consider characters' points of view, discuss character problems and attempts to solve them, identify the moral of the story, or discuss mood and tone. In the context of stories, we often need to make inferences about character's feelings or motivations. Let's look at an example of teacher scaffolding to support making inferences during a storybook read aloud. During a read aloud of *A Frog Thing* (Drachman & Muscarello, 2005), one teacher planned a Raise the Bar question to help students to make inferences about the main character's feelings. After two students responded, the teacher asked additional Raise the Bar questions to get them to use the text and illustrations as evidence for the inferences they made. In this part of the story, Frank, who is a frog, is trying to fly and he is failing miserably. The other frogs are laughing at his attempts.

Teacher: He fell again. How do you think he feels? (Raise the Bar: make inferences about character feelings)
Joshua: Sad.
Emilee: Embarrassed.
Teacher: What makes you think he's sad, Joshua? (Raise the Bar: explain thinking)

Joshua: Because his eyebrows are down and his eyes are . . . his eyes are like (shows using sad facial expression).

Teacher: His eyes are like (sad facial expression). You mean his eyes look sad, huh? So the illustration helped you figure out how he felt.

Teacher: Another idea was embarrassed. Emilee, why do you think he's embarrassed? (Raise the Bar: explain thinking)

Emilee: Because everybody is laughing at him. They think it's funny cuz he's falling and everything.

Teacher: Oh, and is there anything in the illustrations that makes you think he is embarrassed? (Raise the Bar: request to explain thinking and use illustrations as evidence)

Emilee: He's hiding.

Teacher: He tried to fly and it didn't work and now he's hiding under the lily pad. You guys think he's embarrassed *and* sad. Poor Frank. Let's see what happens next.

Although we often plan questions that raise the bar during a read aloud, we also encounter times when a student shows us that he or she needs to be challenged even more. Thus, Raise-the-Bar Strategies are perfect for differentiating instruction for those students who have strong background knowledge or who understand what the text said and need to be challenged to think more deeply about the content. In those instances, we have an opportunity to push a student to even higher levels of cognitive thinking. For example, Emilee in the previous example made an unexpected comparison during that same read aloud of *A Frog Thing* (Drachman & Muscarello, 2005). At this point in the story, a baby bird falls into the water and Frank saves the bird.

Teacher: Look, a little baby bird fell in the water. That's a problem, isn't it? (Raise the Bar: referring to narrative text structure)

Emilee: So Frank's kinda like a baby bird. (Pause) A baby bird can't fly. (Interesting insight)

Teacher: Oh, a baby bird can't fly. You are making a great comparison between Frank and the baby bird! So tell us how Frank is the same as a baby bird and how is he different? (Raise the Bar: compare/contrast within text)

Emilee: He can't fly. (Accurate but not complete and does not use the language of comparisons)

Teacher: So that is how they are the same—neither one can fly. (High Support: model the language of comparison) Let's think about how they are different. Will the bird eventually learn to fly? (High Support: yes/no question)

Emilee: Yeah. When he's older.

Teacher: But will Frank ever learn to fly? (High Support: yes/no question)

Emilee: No.

Teacher: So tell me how Frank is *different* from the bird. (Original Raise the Bar question: contrast)

Emilee: He's a frog and he's a bird (pointing) . . . and, um, Frank's not going to be able to fly. (This response shows Emilee understands the difference between Frank and the baby bird but again does not use the language of a contrast)

Teacher: Yeah, when the *bird* is older, he *will* learn to fly. But *Frank* is a frog, so he *won't* learn to fly. That's how they are different. (High Support: model of the contrast)

The student initiated this interaction by making an excellent observation, comparing Frank (who could not fly) to the baby bird (who also could not fly yet). The teacher capitalized on this observation by asking the student to explain the comparison more fully and to add a contrast of the two characters. Although the student understood these concepts and she improved her response, she still did not use the language of comparisons (e.g., they both/ neither . . .) and contrasts (e.g., the bird . . . but the frog . . .). Therefore, the teacher provided a High Support model of more sophisticated language for each one. This is a good example of how teachers apply various levels of support within one interaction. In this case, the support pushed Emilee further along in her ability to express a complex idea.

Informational Texts

Informational texts provide many opportunities to raise the bar as well. Students can make inferences, connect information to their own lives, compare and contrast, and explain. Informational texts are particularly rich in technical vocabulary; therefore, they provide many opportunities to define new words. When reading informational text, one goal is to be sure students can identify the main idea. In fact, identifying the main idea is a precursor to summarizing and synthesizing information. Let's look at an example of a teacher's scaffolding to help students to identify main ideas in an informational text.

Teacher: We're going to read a couple more sections in our book about dogs and this time I'm not going to decide the important information; I'm going to ask you guys to decide what the important, new information is. Think you're up to that challenge?

Students: Yeah.

Teacher: (Points to and reads the heading and then reads that section)

Teacher: What was the important, new information in that section? What does the author want us to know? (Raise the Bar: author's craft; waits but no response) Okay; turn to your partner and talk about what was important in the book. (Students talk about the section and tell one another what they think was important)

Teacher: Turn back to me in 5, 4, 3, 2, 1. Is there a group that would like to share what the important information was in that section? Nina?

Nina: They're not howling at the moon.

Teacher: They're not howling at the moon? (Low support: repeat student's words to request clarification)

Nina: No, the dogs are talking to each other.

Teacher: So what is the important, new information in this section? What does the author want us to know? (Original Raise the Bar questions: author's craft)

Nina: When dogs howl, they are really talking to each other, not the moon.

Teacher: So the important information is that dogs don't howl at the moon; they howl because they are talking or communicating to each other.

Identifying the main idea in an informational text is an important and often challenging skill for students. Likewise, text features such as graphs and tables can be challenging for students to interpret and often require explicit instruction. In the following example, after reading *What Are Food Chains and Webs?* (Kalman & Langille, 2005), the teacher asks students if they can explain the illustrations of food webs based on what they have just learned from the book.

Teacher: Look at this picture of forest animals (pauses). Now look at this about the ocean animals (pauses). What does this picture tell us? (Raise the Bar: explain text features)

Staci: It tells us what eats what.

Geoff: Oh, I know. The shark eats the fish, and the fish eats the coral and the coral eats . . . (pause)

Teacher: It says zooplankton. The coral eats the zooplankton and the zooplankton eats the phytoplankton (pointing to the pictures). So what do these arrows mean? (Raise the Bar: explain text features)

Geoff: What it eats.

Teacher: What it eats? (Low Support: repeat student's words to request clarification)

Geoff: Yeah, it means the shark eats all those different kinds of fish.

After discussing the forest, ocean, and arctic food webs, the teacher continues discussing the illustrations by pointing to the key and explaining what the symbols mean and how they can be used to interpret the illustration. Informational texts provide many opportunities to raise the bar.

Poetry

We can raise the bar in many of the same ways during poetry read alouds as we can during literature and informational text read alouds. However, poetry offers more opportunities to talk about words and the images they invoke. After listening to the poem "The Wood Frog" (in Florian, 2001) about a hibernating frog, a teacher initiates a discussion about two interesting words the author used in the poem.

> *Teacher:* If the frog is a frogsicle in a logsicle, what do you think the poet was telling us about the frog and the log? (Raise the Bar: author's word choice)
> *Maya:* Well, when you said it was 10 degrees, I can only think of one place that could be that cold—Alaska. Alaska is really cold.
> *Teacher:* Alaska is really, really cold. So think about things that are really cold and about frogsicle and logsicle. What is the poet telling us? (Original Raise the Bar question)
> *Maya:* Oh, they're really cold like a Popsicle!
> *Teacher:* Logsicle, frogsicle, Popsicle. Yes, the author made up those words because they would make us think of the word Popsicle. You got it—the frogs hiding in the log are very cold like Popsicles.

The teacher thought that hearing the words "frogsicle" and "logsicle" would remind students of icicles or Popsicles, and one student did after a few repetitions of the words. Maya noticed the poem was talking about cold weather and then she made the connection between cold, Popsicle, and the two new words.

In another example, the teacher and students have finished discussing Carl Sandburg's poem about fog (www.poetryfoundation.org/poem/174299) and how Sandburg compared the fog to a cat. The teacher told the students that they would be writing a poem about nature and comparing it to something they know. After identifying different items in nature (e.g., rocks, leaves), including types of weather, the teacher asks a question.

> *Teacher:* Maya, you mentioned a tornado. What is something you know that reminds you of a tornado? What could you compare a tornado to? (Raise the Bar: personal connection)
> *Maya:* Kool-Aid. And the reason I said Kool-Aid is whenever I make Kool-Aid with my dad and stir it with a spoon and then take it out, there's a big swirling thing like a tornado.

After students were allowed to make several more comparisons between nature and personal experiences or objects, they were ready to write their own poems.

In a final example, the teacher introduces students to shape or concrete poetry. She hands students a shape poem and asks them what they notice about the poem. Some students begin reading the poem. After a few moments, the teacher asks the students to stop, and she begins a conversation with them by telling them what she noticed about their approach to reading the poem.

> *Teacher:* James, I noticed you were turning your paper to read the poem.
> *James:* Yeah, so I can read the words. Some are sideways.
> *Teacher:* Why did the author write some of the words sideways? (Raise the Bar: explain text features).
> *James:* I don't—oh, because it looks like a tree!
> *Teacher:* What looks like a tree? (Low Support: request clarification)
> *James:* The poem. I mean the words look like branches and these words are the trunk.
> *Tanya:* Hey, my words are the ice cubes in a glass!

While it is tempting to explain a new concept to students, sometimes a simple experience like this one, or a well-placed comment, will provide the scaffolding needed for students to come up with ideas on their own.

SUMMARY

There is no doubt that reading aloud exposes students to new information and ideas. However, it does not guarantee that students are actively processing the content presented in the text. Creating opportunities for rich discussions ensures that students are actively engaged with the content of the text and that they are thinking more deeply about topics or issues. Discussion also provides opportunities to use language to formulate ideas. However, it is particularly important that we provide the right kind of scaffolding to maximize learning. As mentioned, highly skilled teachers make it look easy, but engaging students in meaningful discussions requires practice and thoughtful reflection to improve how we provide responsive-interactive scaffolding. Yet it is well worth our effort when we see more students engaging in discussions, answering challenging questions, making thought-provoking observations, and, of course, enjoying the texts we read aloud. Now let's talk about how to apply these responsive-interactive scaffolding strategies during read alouds using different genres of text.

CHAPTER 5

Literature

According to the Common Core State Standards, children's literature should include picture books, fairy tales, fables, folktales, and novels. Without a doubt, teachers do read such literature aloud to students. We read literature for entertainment as well as to help students learn vocabulary (Beck & McKeown, 2007), conceptual knowledge (Neuman, Pinkham, & Kaefer, 2015), story structure (Lynch & van den Broek, 2007), and listening comprehension (Morrow, 2003). Indeed, good stories can increase the motivation to learn how to read. In short, the journey to becoming a proficient reader involves numerous and meaningful opportunities to hear and interact with increasingly complex texts. There is no doubt that reading and discussing stories with students will help them to make progress toward all 10 of the Reading Standards for Literature that they are expected to achieve, as well as the standards for writing, language, and speaking and listening.

BENEFITS AND CHALLENGES OF READING LITERATURE ALOUD

Reading literature is not all about achieving what is included in the Common Core State Standards! We know that first and foremost, it is fun to read a good story aloud, and it makes us feel good. The shared experiences created by reading a story create common ground for discussions, and they help us to bond with others. Stories can teach us about people and places and help us to think about and communicate our beliefs and values. Finally, because some students come to school with a lot of exposure to stories, whether it is through shared reading of books or through oral traditions of storytelling, students often understand how stories work. Thus, stories can level the playing field for students from different backgrounds and cultures, and teachers can begin using this genre to address a variety of learning objectives.

Because reading literature aloud is a common and enjoyable classroom activity, it may be hard to imagine the challenges that can arise. Nevertheless, literature can present challenges for teachers and students. One challenge that some teachers and students encounter is shifting from a primarily entertainment stance to one that also maximizes the learning potential that quality literature offers. That is not to say that we should not enjoy literature; in fact, all read alouds should be enjoyable. However, when reading for instructional purposes, we need to challenge students to think beyond the routine of sharing highlights, as in "My favorite part was . . ."

Another challenge to reading literature is that students need to listen for durations with few interactions to support them. When we read literature, we typically limit the amount of talk during the read aloud, in part to maintain the flow of the story. While this may not be an issue for some students, it can be frustrating for other students, who may struggle to comprehend, especially if they are discouraged from asking questions. Those students may lose interest in the story. Further, when stories include challenging language or do not follow a typical narrative structure, students may become confused. For example, students may struggle with a story such as *The Day Jimmy's Boa Ate the Wash* (Noble & Kellogg, 1992), which is presented in a backward sequence. Similarly, the figurative language included in *Amelia Bedelia* (Parish & Siebel, 1963) may be confusing, especially to ELLs.

How can we capitalize on the benefits of literature read alouds while minimizing the challenges? The answer is through intentional planning. In this book, we emphasize the need to provide scaffolding—the right kind of scaffolding, in the right amount, at the right time. The decisions we make about the read aloud ahead of time can either *help* our students learn or *hinder* them from doing so. Therefore, planning *is* a form of scaffolding! We recommend the following five steps for planning:

1. Identify the learning objective(s)
2. Choose a text
3. Plan a method for introducing the text
4. Write specific questions to ask or comments to use
5. Select anchor charts and activities

We will discuss each of these in turn.

IDENTIFY THE LEARNING OBJECTIVE(S)

Identifying the learning objective(s) is the first step in planning a literature read aloud. The learning objective might be a Common Core State Standard that you would like to address such as Reading Literature Standard 1.2, which states that students will "describe characters, settings, and major events in a story, using key details" (NGA & CCSSO, 2010, p. 11). Alternatively, learning objectives may come from the required curriculum.

Although learning objectives typically drive the decisionmaking process, sometimes we find a book that we really want to share with our students. In that case, we must decide whether to read it aloud solely for its entertainment value or to identify how to use the book to teach skills or concepts. For example, we enjoy the Mo Willem's Knuffle Bunny series and could easily imagine using the stories to discuss how the author uses photographs and drawings to support his story (e.g., integration of knowledge and ideas).

CHOOSE A TEXT

Learning objectives guide our choices regarding which books to read aloud. Because it is rare for students to learn a skill or a concept the first time we teach it, consider choosing several books that help students achieve the objective. For example, if the learning objective is for students to describe different types of story structures, then we need to read stories that allow them to compare and contrast structure. We could read *A Frog Thing* (Drachman & Muscarello, 2005), which uses a typical linear story structure to tell about Frank, a frog who wants to do more than ordinary frog things. Then we could read *There Was an Old Lady Who Swallowed a Frog!* (Colandro & Lee, 2014), which uses a predictable text pattern. Alternatively, if the objective is for students to learn about figurative language, we could read *New Shoes for Silvia* (Hurwitz & Pinkney, 1993), about a little girl who receives "new shoes that are as red as the inside of a watermelon," and *My Best Friend Is as Sharp as a Pencil: And Other Funny Classroom Portraits* (Piven, 2010), about a girl who gives exciting responses to her grandma's questions about school.

Learning objectives targeting Common Core State Standards will require stories that include sophisticated ideas: books that require students to make predictions, infer character feelings and motivations, make experiential connections, learn new vocabulary, and work to construct meaning (Beck & McKeown, 2001; McGee & Schickedanz, 2007). However, from preschool to 2nd grade, and across students with learning differences, students will vary in their ability to handle the text. Therefore, it is important to choose books carefully. Schwarz et al. (2015) suggest that we consider the following attributes of a storybook:

- *Vocabulary*—How complex is the vocabulary? How many words are unfamiliar?
- *Language complexity*—How complex is the language? How long are sentences?
- *Story structure*—How complex is the story structure in terms of number of characters, clarity of the story sequence, predictability of the story, and the memory load required?
- *Inferencing*—How much inferencing and problem solving are required?
- *Experience*—How familiar are the activities and experiences of characters?
- *Illustrations*—How supportive are the illustrations?

For students with learning differences, there are several considerations that can help them succeed. Choose stories with a main character that has clear goal-directed behavior. Make sure the illustrations match the actions or events portrayed in the text and do not contain too many extraneous details. It helps when the text makes cause-effect relationships explicit (or consider explaining them during the read aloud). Finally, stories that lend themselves to the use of props or re-enactments can support comprehension (see Box 5.1).

The Common Core Standards also provide guidance for choosing texts. They suggest that teachers consider the following three factors to determine text complexity (see NGA & CCSSO, 2010).

1. Quantitative measures that provide a grade level equivalent or a number such as a Lexile (lexile.com/) and are based on factors such as word frequency, the number of syllables in words, and sentence length.
2. Qualitative factors that influence students' ability to read or comprehend a text, such as (a) layers or levels of meaning or purpose, (b) text structure or organization, (c) language conventionality, (d) clarity of language, (e) prior knowledge demands placed on students, including cultural knowledge, and (f) vocabulary.

BOX 5.1. UNIVERSAL STRATEGIES THAT
SUPPORT STUDENTS WITH LEARNING DIFFERENCES

Many strategies we recommend are highly supportive for students with learning differences, including English language learners and students with disabilities. The following strategies are particularly helpful for these students:

- Plan read alouds to go with classroom themes or units.
- Use a variety of genres, including literature, informational texts, and poetry.
- Create opportunities for dialogue during read alouds.
- Encourage retelling of the text.
- Use a responsive style while reading (e.g., follow the students' lead, use comments more than questions, and expand and extend students' sentences).
- Use High-Support and Low-Support Scaffolding strategies that help students achieve more than they are capable of independently.
- Provide rich explanations of vocabulary. Give child-friendly definitions, provide a synonym, use gestures, and use words in a sentence.
- Teach story grammar explicitly.
- Provide visual supports (e.g., Venn diagrams, concept webs, story maps, objects or props related to the text; see ideas for anchor charts and props in this chapter and in Chapters 6, 7, and 8).

3. Qualities of the reader and the task that would influence book choices including (a) students' interests, (b) students' knowledge and experiences, (c) the purpose for reading/listening to the text, and (d) the tasks to be completed in relation to the text.

How do we apply these guidelines as we choose books? To illustrate, we might consider reading aloud *Shortcut* (Crews, 1996), a story about children who decide to take a shortcut home along the train tracks, even though they had been warned to stay off the tracks. Based on a quantitative measure, *Shortcut* has a Lexile level of 210, which is considered to be at a kindergarten to 1st-grade reading level. Based on qualitative measures, it is an easy text for students to comprehend because of its simple story structure. Although the setting, a railroad track that characters walk along, might be unfamiliar to some students, they could easily make personal connections of walking along a path or sidewalk near their home. Despite its simplicity, *Shortcut* has a central message that is more advanced, that is, the importance of listening to adults, and it includes unique vocabulary (e.g., *brier, steep slopes, tussled*). In this example, we considered it an excellent choice because we believed the students would find it interesting and its central message would inspire discussion.

Finally, while we all have our favorite books to read aloud, there are many new quality texts published each year. It is a good idea to talk with colleagues and media specialists and to view the "Choices" reading list published each year by the International Literacy Association (literacyworldwide.org/). Another good resource is the American Library Association (ALA; www.ala.org/alsc/awardsgrants/bookmedia). The ALA website provides information on books that have won various types of awards, including

- The ***John Newbery Medal*** for the most outstanding contribution to children's literature
- The ***Randolph Caldecott Medal*** for the most distinguished American picture book for children
- The ***Coretta Scott King Book Awards*** for an African American author and illustrator
- The ***(Pura) Belpré Medal*** for a Latino writer and illustrator whose children's books best portray and celebrate the Latino cultural experience
- The ***Schneider Family Book Award*** for books that embody an artistic expression of the disability experience for children

Additionally, visit the American Indian Library Association website (ailanet.org/) to learn about books that have won the American Indian Youth Literature Award.

As is evident from the previous resources, it is important that we include multicultural selections, because literature provides students with opportunities to learn about their own culture and other cultures (Louie, 2006), as well as to discuss social issues (Meller, Richardson, & Hatch, 2009). When students are exposed to literature with characters that they can recognize and relate to, they are more likely to engage in literacy activities (Heflin & Barksdale-Ladd, 2001). Further, listening to or reading culturally and linguistically relevant texts supports students' comprehension (McCollin & O'Shea, 2005). It is important to choose books with strong characters that portray the culture accurately, positively, and without stereotypes. For a full set of guidelines and list of books that meet them, see Higgins (n.d.; free access online).

PLAN A METHOD FOR INTRODUCING THE TEXT

The way we introduce a book can make or break our read aloud. Our introduction needs to both generate interest and establish a clear purpose for listening to the book. When deciding how to introduce a text, consider (a) the learning objective, (b) the needs of the students in the class, and (c) the features of the text itself.

First, the learning objective may provide a method for introducing the book. We can introduce the book by describing the learning objective using child-friendly language. Using an example from the Appendix, one of the learning objectives for the second reading of the book *Amazing Grace* (Hoffman & Binch, 1991) includes retelling the story and comparing and contrasting characters' responses to the problem. Before the second read aloud of this story, we can reintroduce it by helping students recall the problem in the story (Grace wanted to be Peter Pan in the class show but some of her classmates said she could not have that role because she is a girl and she is Black). The purpose for the second read aloud then can be explained this way:

> "We are going to read and retell this story today, and talk about how each character—Grace, her mother, and her grandma—responded to the problem. Let's talk about how they felt and what they did in response. So as you listen to the story, pay close attention to how each one responded to that problem."

Notice that establishing a purpose does not need to involve a lengthy discussion!

Second, we should consider the needs of our students. Will students have sufficient background knowledge to understand the story? Will students with learning differences benefit from some preparation for the story? For example, if reading the story *The Great Kapok Tree* (Cherry, 2000), students who have never studied rain forests might need some background information. This story is about a man who enters a rain forest to chop down a tree but he falls asleep and dreams of the creatures of the rain forest pleading with him to let the tree live. To prepare students to listen to this story, we might show a picture of a rain forest and discuss how the animals depend on the trees for food, shelter, and protection.

Third, we may need to introduce the structure of the text itself. Will students be familiar with the type of story? If so, we might give a brief introduction and focus on the problem. For example, if students are familiar with the structure of Jan Brett's books *The Mitten* (Brett, 1996) or *The Hat* (Brett, 1997), they might need only a brief introduction to her book *The Umbrella* (Brett, 2004), which follows the same pattern. For example, in all these books, the illustrations on the border of each page give clues about what will happen next. If students are not familiar with Brett's books, then they may need an introduction that prepares them for this story structure and what to notice in the illustrations. Consequently, our introduction might include a picture walk of several pages to prepare students to notice the border.

WRITE QUESTIONS AND COMMENTS

Planning specific questions and comments ahead of time ensures that students achieve the learning objective of a read aloud. Also, because we should read some books multiple times, some questions or comments will be better suited for a first, second, or third read aloud. Thus, while planning, it is helpful to map out questions and comments appropriate for each repeated reading.

Our questions and comments need to include a combination of low and high levels of cognitive thinking. But how many should be at low levels of cognitive thinking and how many should be at high levels? For preschool-age students, one recommendation has been to aim for a ratio of 60% at low levels of cognitive thinking, and 40% at high levels of cognitive thinking because that ratio aligns with what happens naturally during book reading interactions (Hammett, van Kleeck, & Huberty, 2003; for discussion, see van Kleeck, 2014). Similarly, Taylor, Pearson, Clark, and Walpole (1999) have found that for accomplished elementary school teachers, 31% of their questions were at high levels of cognitive thinking. Therefore, as we plan for interaction during a read aloud, it seems reasonable to aim for a ratio of 60% at low levels and 40% at high levels of cognitive thinking. Figure 3.3 provides ideas for Raise-the-Bar Strategies for literature texts, and these can help us generate questions and comments at high levels of cognitive thinking prior to the read aloud.

Of course, we also can adjust that ratio to match the needs of our students. We can consider the text complexity, the genre of the text, our students' background knowledge and learning needs, and our learning objectives for the unit and the specific read aloud. For example, if students have limited language abilities or have limited familiarity with the content, we might choose a higher ratio of questions and comments at low levels of cognitive thinking. Alternatively, if students need a greater challenge, we can consider a higher ratio of high levels of cognitive thinking. Remember that students who are ELLs or who have disabilities also should be asked and expected to respond to questions requiring high levels of levels of cognitive thinking. While they may struggle with the language required to respond, they still need opportunities to discuss topics at high levels of cognitive thinking (see Chapter 9 for more ways to support these students).

Writing questions and comments on sticky notes and placing them in the book helps us recall where to initiate a discussion and to stay focused on the purpose for each reading. Thus, when a student initiates a conversation that will lead the discussion away from the learning objective, we are in a better position to decide whether that will be a fruitful discussion and one worth pursuing, or if we wish to stick with our original plan. In this way, our preplanned questions and comments help us be more thoughtful in how we respond to students' contributions. The Appendix includes examples of preplanned questions for each of the chosen texts.

SELECT ANCHOR CHARTS AND ACTIVITIES

The last step in the planning process for a read aloud is to select anchor charts and extension activities that encourage deeper thinking about the book. Anchor charts and activities provide another way to build scaffolding into the read aloud that can increase student success. Anchor charts also help us stay focused on the learning objectives of the read aloud. Extension activities help students to make personal connections with the story, which in turn supports learning. Extension activities also lend themselves to connections across content areas such as social studies, math, science, and technology.

In this section, we present anchor charts and activities that support the Common Core Reading Standards for Literature (i.e., Key Ideas and Details, Craft and Structure, Integration of Knowledge and Ideas), as well as Language and Writing. However, we do not include specific activities to address the Speaking and Listening Standards because these can be addressed during all read alouds and with all these activities. To achieve Speaking and Listening Standards, students need to

- Participate in collaborative conversations, follow agreed-upon rules for discussions, build on the talk of others, and speak clearly and coherently

- Ask and answer questions to clarify or gather additional information, or to deepen understanding
- Describe people, places, things, and events, and express ideas and feelings clearly
- Tell a story or recount an experience with appropriate facts and relevant information
- Add drawings or other visual displays to clarify ideas, thoughts, and feelings
- Produce complete sentences when appropriate (Grades 1–2)
- Create audio recordings of stories or poems (Grade 2)

Similarly, we do not include activities to support Foundational Skills. We certainly could target skills like print concepts or phonological awareness during read alouds (see McGinty, Sofka, Sutton, & Justice, 2006; Price & Ruscher, 2006), and we do suggest some when reading poetry aloud (see Chapter 7). However, here we emphasize ways to foster language, comprehension, and thinking during literature read alouds.

Finally, while it is beyond the scope of this book to address every grade-specific standard, we present activities that we believe can be modified to meet the diverse needs of students from preschool to 2nd grade.

Activities to Target Key Ideas and Details

To achieve Key Ideas and Details of the Reading Standards for Literature, students need to

- Ask and answer who, what, where, when, why, and how questions to show understanding of key ideas and details
- Recall or recount different types of stories, including, for 2nd-graders, the lesson or moral
- Identify and describe the characters, settings, and major events in a story and, for 2nd-graders, describe how characters in a story respond to events and obstacles

Here are two activities addressing these standards.

Story sequence cards. Pictures support sequencing of events in a story, understanding of its structure, and retelling. Some story sequencing cards can be purchased for popular stories; alternatively, we can photocopy several pictures from the book that show the characters, main events, and resolution. Slip photocopies into plastic page covers, ask students to hang them in order on a string with clothespins, and then retell the story. For an extension activity, students can draw key scenes to create a pictograph or storyboard.

Pictographs include just the basics; discourage students from drawing details that take too much time to draw (see Ukrainetz, 1998). Students can use their drawings or the sequence cards to write about the story or to dictate the story to an adult, which supports the writing standards and vocabulary development (Christ, Wang, & Chiu, 2011). Linear stories lend themselves to sequencing; here are a few examples:

Lovell, P., & Catrow, D. (2001). *Stand Tall, Molly Lou Melon*. New York, NY: G. P. Putnam's Sons.

> This delightful story is about Molly Lou, a little girl who has a way of turning faults into talents.

O'Neill, A., & Huliks-Bieth, L. (2002). *The Recess Queen*. New York, NY: Scholastic Press.

> Mean Jean was Recess Queen and a bully, until a new kid arrives at school and becomes Jean's friend.

Shannon, D. (2004). *A Bad Case of the Stripes*. New York, NY: Scholastic Press.

> Camilla Cream worries about what others think of her and she tries to please everyone. In the process, she learns an important lesson.

Story grammar anchor chart. Identifying story grammar elements (characters, setting, goal/problem, actions to obtain goal or attempts to solve problem, and the resolution) supports the recounting of the story. Students use the story grammar elements to retell key ideas and details, while also learning the goals of craft and structure. Create an anchor chart (there are many examples available on the Internet) and ask the following guiding questions:

- Who is the main character?
- Where and when does the story take place?
- What is the main character's goal or problem?
- Why does the character feel the way he or she does?
- What was the character's plan to obtain the goal or solve the problem?
- Why did the character say/do that?
- How was the goal achieved or problem solved?

While many stories we read follow a typical narrative structure, such as fairytales (e.g., *The Princess and the Pea*, Andersen & Dusikova, 2012) and fables (e.g., *The Tortoise and the Hare*, Pinkney, 2013), not all stories follow this structure. Exposing students to a wide array of story structures will teach them to understand and enjoy different formats (which also addresses Craft and Structure standards). Here are a few stories to consider for addressing alternative story structures:

Hall, D., & Cooney, B. (1993). *Ox-Cart Man*. New York, NY: Puffin Books.

This is a circular story about a farmer who fills his cart with products that his family has made and produce they have grown. Then he travels into town to sells his wares. Afterwards, he returns home to begin the cycle of making, growing, and selling again.

James, S. (1996). *Dear Mr. Blueberry*. New York, NY: Aladdin.

Written in letter format, this story tells of Emily, who is corresponding with her teacher, Mr. Blueberry, about a blue whale she discovers living in her pond over summer vacation.

Noble, T. H., & Kellogg, S. (1992). *The Day Jimmy's Boa Ate the Wash*. New York, NY: Puffin Books.

In this story, a little girl tells her mother about a class field trip to the farm. Rather than describing the events in the order in which they happened, the girl begins her story toward the end of the trip and tells a series of ridiculous cause-effect events that all started because Jimmy brought his pet boa constrictor on the class trip.

Activities to Target Craft and Structure

To achieve Craft and Structure standards, students need to

- Ask and answer questions about unknown words and identify and describe how words and phrases suggest or supply meaning
- Recognize common genres, explain major differences between storybook and informational text, and describe the overall structure of a story
- Name the author and illustrator of a story and define the role of each, identify who is telling a story, and acknowledge differences in characters' points of view

Here are three activities targeting these standards.

Vocabulary connections chart. Children's literature contains a wealth of interesting words. Before reading, identify unfamiliar vocabulary that is important for comprehending the story. After reading the text, revisit those vocabulary words and show students how to use context clues to determine a word's meaning. A caution: Not all words will have sufficient context clues to determine the meaning, so be prepared to give child-friendly definitions. Ask students how they might use the word in their own lives. Such text-to-self connections help students retain new words. Figure 5.1 shows an example of a vocabulary connections chart focusing on verbs after reading

Figure 5.1. Example of a Vocabulary Connections Anchor Chart

Using Target Words from *A Frog Thing*

Word	Sentence	Definition	Synonym	How We Would Use the Word
Leap/Leapt	Frank leapt into the air.	Quickly jump or spring	Jump, spring	We like to play the leapfrog game.
Dive/Dove	Frank dove into the water.	To plunge downward	Leap, jump, plunge	We can dive off a diving board. My dad can make his remote control airplane dive in the air.
Wheeze/ Wheezed	Frank wheezed after trying so hard to fly.	To breathe noisily	Gasp, pant	When we run a long way and get out of breath we might wheeze. Sometimes I wheeze because I have asthma.

A Frog Thing (Drachman & Muscarello, 2005). The chart was also created on an iPad to show students how to access an online dictionary while discussing the words.

Character point-of-view anchor chart. Recognizing that characters have different points of view helps students understand characters' feeling, motives, and actions. After discussing a story, revisit it from the viewpoint of different characters. Document the characters' feelings or opinions based on evidence from the text (see Figure 5.2). Acting out a story is another way students can view events from a particular character's point of view. Further, it adds visual, tactual, and kinesthetic input to the language and thinking of the characters. Similarly, Hot Seat (Wilhelm, 2013) is a role-playing activity that helps students understand a character's point of view. When a student is in the "hot seat," he or she answers questions from the character's perspective, including raise the bar questions such as his or her opinion on different topics clearly important to that character. By assuming the persona of a character, students will have a better understanding of what drives the character and the story from the character's point of view.

These books have characters with clearly different points of view:

Browne, A. (2001). *Voices in the Park*. New York, NY: DK Children.

This story allows you to consider a day in the park from four points of view: Charles's mother, Smudge's father, Charles, and Smudge.

Van Allsburg, C. (1988). *Two Bad Ants*. Boston, MA: Houghton Mifflin.

> After a troop of ants raid sugar from a kitchen, two greedy ants stay and have quite an adventure. Consider the adventure and situations from the ants' point of view and a person's point of view.

Young, E. (2002). *Seven Blind Mice*. New York, NY: Puffin.

> Based on a classic Indian tale, seven blind mice each investigate a strange object and then report a different theory about it.

Also, we can compare and contrast common fairytales or books written from various characters' perspectives, such as

Andersen, H. C., & Dusikova, M. (2012). *The Princess and the Pea*. Edinburgh, UK: Floris Books; and Grey, M. (2004). *The Pea and the Princess*. London: Red Fox.

Piumini, R., & Ligi, R. (2009). *Cinderella*. North Mankato, MN: Picture Window Books; and Shaskan, T. S., & Guelais, G. (2011). *Seriously, Cinderella Is SO Annoying!: The Story of Cinderella as Told by the Wicked Stepmother*. North Mankato, MN: Picture Window Books.

Activities to Target Integration of Knowledge and Ideas

To achieve Integration of Knowledge and Ideas standards for reading literature, students need to

- Describe the relationship between illustrations and the story and use illustrations and details to describe and demonstrate understanding of the characters, setting, or plot
- Compare and contrast the adventures and experiences of characters in familiar stories and different versions of the same story

Figure 5.2. Example of a Character's Point of View Anchor Chart

For: Cannon, J. (1993). *Stellaluna*. Boston, MA: Houghton Mifflin.

Character	Eating Bugs	Sleeping	Flying
Stellaluna	Thinks eating bugs is disgusting	Thinks sleeping is best done upside-down hanging by toes	Thinks flying is done at night
Baby birds	Think bugs are delicious	Think sleeping is best done lying in a nest	Think flying is done during the day because it's too dark and scary to fly at night
Mother Bird	Thinks bugs are healthy for her babies	Thinks hanging upside-down to sleep is dangerous	Thinks babies should not fly at night because it's dangerous

Here are two activities that target these standards.

I see, you see. Drawing pictures helps students to attend more closely to the text. Tell students that they will be drawing a picture based on a portion of text you read aloud. Read the text once without showing the illustrations so students can begin visualizing an image and then read the text slowly, pausing at times, so that students can draw their picture. Have students share and explain their pictures, and then compare students' drawings with those in the book. Discuss similarities and differences. Also, ask students to consider how the details in the text were included in the illustrations, how details in the illustration add more information to the story, or both. Prepare students for this activity by reading *Delia's Dull Day* (Myer, 2012) and noticing the amazing things happening in the illustrations that Delia fails to notice and that are not discussed in the text. A few stories that work well for this activity include:

Mazer, A. (1994). *The Salamander Room.* New York, NY: Dragonfly Books.

> A boy finds a salamander in the woods and imagines how he can turn his room into a perfect salamander home.

Palaniti, M., & Fine, F. (1997). *Piggie Pie.* Boston, MA: Houghton Mifflin.

> Gritch, the witch, wants to make piggie pie, but she is missing one critical ingredient—the pigs!

Venn diagrams. Comparing and contrasting facilitates deeper comprehension of ideas within and across texts. Use a Venn diagram to compare and contrast story grammar elements within or across stories, or even to compare ourselves to a character. Below is an example comparing and contrasting two stories by Kevin Henkes (see Figure 5.3):

Henkes, K. (2006). *Lilly's Purple Plastic Purse.* New York, NY: Greenwillow Books.

Henkes, K. (2006). *Lilly's Big Day.* New York, NY: Greenwillow Books.

Venn diagrams are useful with other genres as well.

Finally, while the following activities do not fit neatly under any particular standard, they are important for comprehending literature, as well as other genres, and for developing higher-level thinking skills.

It says, I say, and so . . . making inferences anchor chart. When making inferences, we use context clues and background knowledge to make informed guesses or draw conclusions that are not explicitly stated. When making inferences, we are actively engaged and thinking deeply about the text, and we are more aware of the author's purpose (van Kleeck, 2008). The "It Says . . . I Say . . . And So . . ." anchor chart (Beers, 2003; see Figure 5.4) supports making

Figure 5.3. Example of a Venn Diagram

Comparing *Lilly's Purple Plastic Purse* to *Lilly's Big Day*

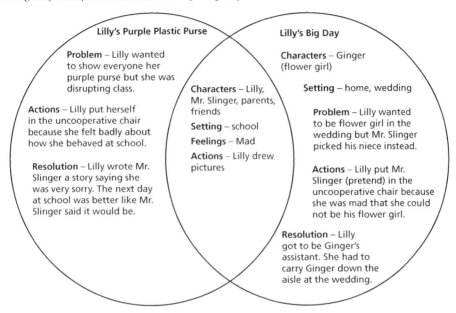

inferences. Prior to the read aloud, identify key questions that will help students focus on important ideas or concepts and that require that they make inferences. For example, read *A Camping Spree with Mr. McGee* (Van Dusen, 2003), a story about Mr. Magee and his dog enjoying a quiet camping trip when suddenly they find themselves plummeting down a mountain in their camper. Help students to attend to and understand the details to consider

Figure 5.4. Example of an It Says . . . I Say . . . And So . . . Anchor Chart

For: Van Dusen, C. (2003). *A Camping Spree with Mr. McGee*. San Francisco, CA: Chronicle Books.

Question	It Says . . .	I Say . . .	And So . . .
1. Why does Mr. Magee want to go camping?	He packed the camper, hit the road, drove to the mountains	Camping is fun No TV, so you play outside	I think Mr. Magee is going on vacation to relax
2. Why is the bear snooping around the camper?	The bear smelled the marshmallows and he wanted a treat	Bears and people don't mix well Bears are dangerous	My guess is that there is going to be a problem
3. Do you think Mr. Magee will go camping again?	He camped in the backyard with his dog	Camping isn't fun when there are bears	I conclude that Mr. Magee won't go camping in the mountains

what might happen next and why. For example, help them use the following sentence starters:

- I infer that . . .
- I think that . . .
- My guess is that . . .
- My conclusion here is . . .

In addition to wordless picture books, images, and short videos (e.g., Pixar), these books support making inferences:

Nolen, J., & Catrow, D. (2005). *Plantzilla*. Boston, MA: Houghton Mifflin.

At the end of the school year, Mortimer takes a plant home. Throughout the summer, Plantzilla continues to grow, strange things begin to happen, and his quiet is disrupted.

Stock, C. (1993). *Where Are You Going, Manyoni?* New York, NY: Morrow Junior Books.

This story of a young girl, Manyoni, and her long walk to school in rural Zimbabwe will delight students and help them to make inferences about unfamiliar vocabulary.

Van Allsburg, C. (1986). *The Stranger*. Boston, MA: Houghton Mifflin.

A story about a farmer who, after he accidentally hits a stranger with his truck, brings the man home to help him to get better. The farmer begins to wonder if the stranger might actually be Jack Frost due to his odd relationship with the weather.

Making connections anchor chart. Good readers make connections to the text. There are three types of connections readers might make to the text: (a) to their own personal experiences (text-to-self), (b) to other texts that they have read (text-to-text), or (c) to happenings in the real world (text-to-world) (Harvey & Goudvis, 2007). Such connections increase active engagement during read alouds. Use a making connections anchor chart to model these types of connections. Figure 5.5 includes an example anchor chart. We also use a laminated blank copy of this chart to fill in during read alouds. The following questions can guide students to make connections:

- Has something like this happened to you in your life? (text-to-self)
- What feelings did you have when you read this text? (text-to-self)
- Does this remind you of another book you have read? (text-to-text)
- How is it similar to another book you have read? How is it different? (text-to-text)

Figure 5.5. Example of a Making Connections Anchor Chart

Text-to-Self	When it said _____, it reminded me of . . .
	I am like this character because . . .
	I am different from this character because . . .
	In my own life, I . . .
Text-to-Text	This book reminds me of another book that I read because . . .
	This character is like another character in _____ book I read because . . .
	This character has a problem that is similar to the problem in _____ (book) because . . .
	The setting in this story is similar to the setting in _____ (book) because . . .
Text-to-World	This book reminds me of _____ that happened in history because . . .
	When _____ happened it reminded me of _____ because . . .
	I know about this because . . .
Text-to-Media	This book reminds me of something I saw on TV, read on the computer, or heard in a song because . . .

- How is it similar to a video, movie, or TV show you have watched? How is it different? (text-to-text)
- What does this remind you of in the real world? (text-to-world)

Activities to Target Language Standards

To achieve Language Standards, students need to

- Demonstrate the conventions of Standard English grammar when writing or speaking
- Demonstrate conventions of Standard English capitalization, punctuation, and spelling when writing
- Determine or clarify the meaning of unknown and multiple-meaning words and phrases
- Explore or demonstrate the understanding of word relationships and nuances in word meanings
- Use words and phrases acquired through conversations, read alouds, and readings

During read alouds of all genres, there are opportunities to create respectful conversations that help students express their ideas clearly using conventions of Standard English grammar. Stories themselves provide a model for correct use of pronouns (e.g., *he, she, him, her, myself*), irregular plural nouns (e.g., *feet, mice, men*), regular past tense verbs (e.g., *grabbed*), auxiliary verbs (e.g., *could* see, *was* safe, *had* burned), and irregular verbs (e.g., *told, found, bought*). Further, there are opportunities to teach sophisticated vocabulary from stories. The following two activities support these language standards.

Props and prop boxes. Props create interest in a story, and prop boxes can be used to extend learning and conversations after the read aloud. For preschool or kindergarten students, provide materials to use to reenact the story and allow for student-directed play. For example, for a *Strega Nona* (DePaola, 1975) prop box, include realistic props like a paper bag vest, a scarf and apron, a broom and dustpan, and forks and bowls, as well as symbolic props like a cardboard tube, cut rubber bands, and a round basket (Welsch, 2008). Symbolic props encourage imaginative play that goes beyond the story and cooperation with peers as they consider ways to use them. For 1st- or 2nd-grade students, a prop box can support dramatization of a play based on a script they have been given or they have written, much like Readers' Theatre. Writing a script aligns with the Writing Standards, while reading it supports fluency for Foundational Skills.

Figurative language anchor chart. Figurative language helps to create clear or powerful images about a situation. However, figurative language can be confusing, because the words and phrases do not mean exactly what they say. To teach figurative language, identify the types of language used in a text, provide a brief definition, and give examples. For instance, a simile is a comparison using "like" or "as." Examples include "*busy as a bee*" or "*sly as a fox*." A metaphor is a comparison stated as a fact. For example, "*You are what you eat*" and "*He is a shining star*" are both metaphors.

Many stories and poems (see Chapter 7) use figurative language. The following stories contain similes, metaphors, or both:

Leedy, L. (2009). *Crazy Like a Fox: A Simile Story*. New York, NY: Holiday House.

This story is about Rufus, the fox, and Babette, the sheep, and it is told with similes such as Rufus "sleeping like a log" and "running as fast as lighting."

Yolen, J. (1987). *Owl Moon*. New York, NY: Philomel Books.

A girl and her father go in search of the Great Horned Owl on a moonlit winter night.

These books include personification or give an animal or object human-like characteristics:

Edwards, P. D. (2009). *The Old House*. New York, NY: Puffin Books.

An old house longs to have a family living inside it, but it looks so sad and miserable that people who come to look at it usually leave again.

Rathmann, P. (1995). *Officer Buckle and Gloria*. New York, NY: G.P. Putnam's Sons Books for Young Readers.

> Officer Buckle is dedicated to teaching children about safety, but his talks are boring until he brings along his dog, Gloria.

Finally, these books contain idioms or phrases that have a different meaning from that of the actual words used:

Arnold, T. (2003). *More Parts*. New York, NY: Puffin Books; and Arnold, T. (2007). *Even More Parts*. New York, NY: Puffin Books.

> Filled with idioms such as "hold your tongue" and "I lost my head" that leave Chip Block, the hero of the story, a bit nervous, but will certainly delight young students.

Parish, P., & Siebel, F. (1963). *Amelia Bedelia*. New York, NY: Greenwillow Books.

> Amelia Bedelia follows directions, but following them literally leads to hilarious results.

Activities to Target Writing

Writing helps students to think more deeply about ideas, concepts, and topics. To achieve the Writing Standards, students need to

- Use a combination of drawing, dictating (kindergarten), and writing (kindergarten through 2nd grade) to compose opinion pieces, informative/explanatory texts, and narratives
- Focus on a topic, strengthen writing, and use a variety of digital tools, with guidance and support
- Participate in shared research and writing projects

Activities to target writing also can address other standards described above. We suggest the following two activities.

Somebody-Wanted-but-So-Then anchor chart. Summarizing is important and one strategy that helps students to write a summary is called "Somebody-Wanted-but-So-Then" (see Figure 5.6; Beers, 2003). By completing this anchor chart, students can recognize, discuss, and then write about the relationship between the main characters, the goal, the problem, the attempts, and the resolution of the story. As you read a story aloud, ask these guiding questions and fill in the sections of the chart:

- **Somebody:** Who is a main character?
- **Wanted:** What does he or she want or need in this story?

Figure 5.6. Example of a Somebody-Wanted-but-So-Then Anchor Chart

For: Henkes, K. (1993). *Owen*. New York, NY: Greenwillow Books.

Somebody	Wanted	But	So	Then
(Main characters)	(Goal/ Motivation)	(Conflict/ Reason)	(Attempt)	(Resolution)
Owen	Wanted to keep his special fuzzy yellow blanket forever	But his parents try different ways to get him to let it go	So Owen hides it so the "blanket fairy" won't get it He picks a new favorite corner when his parents try the "vinegar trick"	Finally Owen's mother cuts the blanket up and sews handkerchiefs that Owen can take wherever he goes

- **But:** But what gets in the way of the character getting what she or he wants or needs?
- **So:** So what does she or he do about it?
- **Then:** Then what happened?

Letter-writing. Although emails and text messages are common forms of communication, letter-writing should be encouraged as well, because it teaches good social skills. The class or individual students can write thank-you letters after a field trip or to someone who visited the class. Letters can also be written to an expert to request more information about a topic or to an author or illustrator (resources for contacting authors and illustrators: www.carolhurst.com/authors/authors.html; www.scholastic.com/teacher/ab/biolist.htm). Further, students can engage in creative writing by writing a letter to a character or writing a letter as if they were that character. The following books are written in letter format, which might inspire students to write letters.

Ada, A. F., & Tyron, L. (2004). *With Love, Little Red Hen*. New York, NY: Atheneum Books for Young Readers.

> Little Red Hen and her seven little chicks have recently moved into a cottage in Hidden Forest. To get to know her neighbors and to encourage them to help her with her work, Little Red Hen writes letters to her neighbors.

Rakusin, S. (2000). *Dear Calla Roo . . . Love, Savannah Blue*. Carrboro, NC: Winged Willow Press.

> Savannah Blue, a Great Dane, and Calla Ruth, a little girl, have become new friends. However, because they live far away from each other they become pen pals to stay close.

Teague, M. (2003). *Dear Mrs. LaRue: Letters from Obedience School*. New York, NY: Scholastic.

> Not happy to be attending Obedience School, a dog laments his fate in a series of letters home.

Stewart, S., & Small, D. (1997). *The Gardener*. New York, NY: Farrar Straus Giroux.

> During the Depression, Lydia Grace goes to the city to stay with her cantankerous uncle. The story is told through Lydia's letters written home in which she describes how she changes her uncle's bakery, and his spirit, by growing flowers the way her grandmother taught her.

SUMMARY

In this chapter, we considered the benefits and challenges of reading literature aloud to students and described ways to plan for a read aloud in order to minimize the challenges and maximize learning. We considered the types of questions and comments to plan, including how many at low levels versus high levels of cognitive thinking. Finally, we described a variety of anchor charts and activities to structure or extend the discussions during read alouds in order to address the Common Core State Standards.

CHAPTER 6

Informational Texts

In the era of the CCSS, informational texts have a much more prominent place in instructional contexts in the classroom. In fact, the CCSS state:

> Classroom teachers can infuse the English language arts block with rich, age-appropriate content knowledge and vocabulary in history/social studies, science, and the arts [, and] having students listen to informational read-alouds in the early grades helps lay the necessary foundation for students' reading and understanding of increasingly complex texts on their own in subsequent grades (NGA & CCSSO, 2010, p. 33).

Thus, teachers can incorporate informational texts from various disciplines into their read alouds. Informational texts can include concept books, how-to books, and magazines, as well as books that describe, sequence, or compare and contrast information. Reading aloud and discussing informational texts with students will help them to make progress toward the Reading Standards for Informational Texts, as well as standards for writing, speaking and listening, and language.

BENEFITS AND CHALLENGES OF INFORMATIONAL TEXT READ ALOUDS

There are many benefits to reading informational text to students. Having informational texts read aloud teaches students about the world around them, about other people and places, and about history and science. Informational texts inspire students to learn more by asking questions and making comments. Likewise, they inspire teachers to engage in more discussions that help students understand content. In fact, discussions occur more frequently when teachers read informational texts aloud compared with reading storybooks aloud. In addition, the content of these discussions tends to be at high levels of cognitive thinking, such as explaining, defining, comparing, or relating to real-life experiences. Such discussions are an effective means for deepening knowledge of a topic; learning new information; and strengthening speaking, listening, and language skills. Further, a read aloud serves as a community-building activity that allows all students, regardless of their reading abilities, to share a common experience. Therefore, a read aloud, and the discussion it inspires, becomes a cornerstone for teaching content and academic vocabulary to a class.

Reading informational texts is beneficial for our students, but the reality is that we experience a number of challenges with this genre. Informational texts are dense with content. Therefore, we talk more during the read aloud to explain concepts and facts that may or may not be explained fully within the text and that students may or may not be familiar with already. Also, compared with storybooks, informational texts can be grammatically complex and include more unfamiliar vocabulary. Consequently, we add explanations to help students understand the language. Even the illustrations can be more challenging than those included in storybooks. Illustrations such as drawings, diagrams, charts, or text boxes may be helpful for explaining the content, but they require us to make many decisions, such as when to read the text and when to explain an illustration, how to use the illustration in our explanation, or how to determine if we should explain an illustration now or during a second reading. Regardless, at some point we must teach students to interpret the illustrations and relate them to the text. In addition, students initiate more talk during informational text read alouds compared to storybook read alouds, often because they are curious about the topic and interested in the illustrations.

All this results in a high amount of talk during the read aloud, which can be challenging. We must decide when to explain something, how to answer students' questions and integrate their comments, and how to manage the flow of talk. We may need to manage behavior more often when reading aloud an informational text compared to a storybook. For example, we may need to more frequently tell students what is expected (e.g., "Listen quietly to this page before we talk about it" or "Raise your hand when you have an idea"). All this talk can extend the duration of the read aloud beyond some students' ability to attend to the task. Therefore, during the read aloud we have to monitor students' attention and interest in the text. While the goal is to achieve the instructional objective, we may need to end the read aloud before students lose interest.

Clearly, reading informational texts aloud can be challenging! However, the challenges can be managed by planning ahead and by using the responsive-interactive scaffolding strategies during the read aloud to manage the talk. Having a good plan actually helps us manage the flow of talk during the read aloud; therefore, it is the first step toward scaffolding our students' success. Planning does not need to be time consuming because, in part, learning objectives and texts may be part of a curriculum. In that case, our planning is more about deciding how to use those suggested texts or identifying other texts to support the objectives.

Planning includes the same five steps outlined for literature read alouds:

1. Identify the learning objective(s)
2. Choose a text
3. Plan a method for introducing the text
4. Write questions and comments to use
5. Select anchor charts and activities

IDENTIFY THE LEARNING OBJECTIVE(S)

Identifying learning objectives for the read aloud is important for maximizing the learning potential of the discussion and managing the interactions. When a read aloud occurs within a broader context of a unit, identifying the learning objective for a specific read aloud follows on the unit goals and objectives. Situating the read aloud within a unit is ideal because vocabulary and concepts can be encountered multiple times across multiple contexts (e.g., science or social studies, reading, writing, art, play). Such exposure enables a cyclical process of deeper and deeper learning (Lipson, Valencia, Wixson, & Peters, 1993).

For example, we know two teachers who integrated two information books and a storybook within their science unit on frogs. The teachers wanted students to achieve three learning objectives:

- To identify healthy habitats for frogs
- To retell the life cycle of frogs
- To recognize differences between storybook and informational text genres

These concepts guided their choices about texts, the question they asked, and the activities they planned. They taught specific vocabulary and content during read alouds and also during other instructional activities such as science inquiry, writing, and drawing. For example, students observed and documented the changes in tadpoles in an aquarium in the classroom. They considered the physical environments where different species of frogs live, including exploring their own school and home surroundings. They discussed what frogs needed to survive (e.g., food, safe habitats, protection from predators) and compared those needs to their own needs. The two informational texts included features typical of the genre, while in the storybook about frogs, the animal characters were talking to one another. The teachers took the opportunity to talk about factual text versus fictional text, and contrast the text and illustrations in the two genres. The read alouds had an important role in instruction, and students made connections across texts, across disciplines, and across activities over several weeks.

CHOOSE A TEXT

Choosing texts follows the learning objectives. Look for texts that contain the specific information needed for teaching the topic. For example, if the learning objective includes the Common Core Standard comparing texts on the same topic (kindergarten, 1st grade) or identifying important points in two texts on the same topic (2nd grade), then find two informational texts on the topic that will lend themselves to comparing similarities and differences in content and text features (e.g., table of contents, headings, captions, graphs, tables, glossary).

The availability of good informational texts appropriate for students in preschool to 2nd grade has increased substantially over the past decade. However, given a particular age group or topic unit, choosing texts can sometimes be difficult. Thus, consider the following attributes when choosing texts (Price & Bradley, 2011):

- *Vocabulary*—How complex is the vocabulary? How many words are unfamiliar? Does the text include simple explanations of those words? Are those words supported by the illustrations?
- *Content*—How familiar is the content? Will the text be used to teach new content, or to support and enhance students' current knowledge?
- *Language complexity*—How complex is the language? How long are sentences?
- *Illustration support*—How supportive are the illustrations? Do they include real photographs or clear drawings? Do graphs, diagrams, and so on provide clear explanations?
- *Print features*—How large and clear is the font? Where is the text located? Is it on a consistent location on each page?
- *Text genre*—Is the text strictly informational? Is it a hybrid that includes story features? Hybrid texts can place information within a context that students can understand more easily, and thus be facilitative. However, the mixing of text genres also can confuse students. Hybrids that include separate information and story lines can be challenging for teachers to read aloud.

Sometimes we locate a text that is less than ideal but is useful for our instructional purpose. In that case, we need methods to overcome the less desirable features. For example, one teacher choosing texts for the frog unit thought one text contained excellent information, illustrations, vocabulary, and sentence complexity. However, the book was too long and contained distracting text box insertions. The teacher managed those challenges by choosing to read only the segments that fit the learning objectives and by covering distracting text boxes with sticky notes. Those strategies helped the teacher manage the duration of the read aloud and keep it focused on the target content.

Students with learning differences will be more successful when we keep a few guidelines in mind when selecting informational texts. Keep the amount of information on a page manageable and make sure to limit the number of unknown words. Consider texts with short, simple sentences and with illustrations that support the text. Photographs that isolate important details are better than those that include detailed backgrounds. Also, consider the type of information text genre. Consider whether using hybrid texts (those that contain both story and informational text characteristics) is a good idea. For students who struggle with story structure or with inferring character feelings or perspectives, hybrid texts make comprehension more challenging. Therefore, it would be better to use texts that are strictly informational. Conversely, for students who exhibit a strength in comprehending stories, hybrid texts with their storylike features can facilitate comprehension while introducing students to informational text features. See Box 6.1 for other ideas for planning for students with learning differences.

Finally, in Chapter 5, we presented guidelines and resources for choosing stories. In addition to those, we recommend that you use resources provided by the Children's Book Council (CBC; www.cbcbooks.org/), the National Science Teachers Association (NSTA; www.nsta.org/), and the National Council for the Social Studies (NCSS; www.socialstudies.org/). Each year the CBC works in cooperation with the NSTA to identify outstanding science trade books, and with the NCSS to identify notable social studies trade books for young people. Both lists include high-quality books appropriate to read aloud to students in preschool through 2nd grade.

PLAN A METHOD FOR INTRODUCING THE TEXT

Next we want to decide how to introduce the text so that we generate interest and establish a clear purpose. Identifying a purpose will help students focus their attention during the read aloud. More important, perhaps, having a clear purpose also helps us manage the talk that occurs during the read aloud. When students make comments and ask questions that take the discussion in a direction different from that of our planned purpose, we have a decision to make. We can either follow the students in an unplanned direction to capitalize on their curiosity or to correct a misunderstanding, or we can stay the course and guide the discussion back to our original purpose. For example, the learning objectives for a science unit on frogs helped one teacher respond to students' initiations during each read aloud. When a student initiated a conversation about seeing frogs smashed on the road, the teacher helped connect

---

BOX 6.1. PLANNING AHEAD FOR STUDENTS WITH LEARNING DIFFERENCES

As you plan for read alouds, consider the types of students in your classroom. The following considerations can help you support students with learning differences. For further description, see Chapter 9.

- Consider the needs of students with learning differences when choosing books to read aloud.
- Plan for repeated exposure to the text for all students, but especially for students with learning differences.
- Consider seating options that will maximize students' attention.
- Consider reading to students with learning differences in small groups, either prior to the classroom read aloud or following it.
- Preteach selected vocabulary (for ideas on selecting vocabulary, see Neuman & Wright, 2013). Target vocabulary words for students with learning differences may be different from the words chosen for the rest of the class. Plan multiple opportunities to use these words throughout the day across activities.
- Plan opportunities for students with learning differences to interact during the read aloud. Plan ahead for ways to provide High Support for students who will need it.
- Plan questions to initiate discussions at high levels of cognitive demand. Remember that students with learning differences often are capable of thinking at high levels even though they may struggle with the language to express those high-level ideas. Asking only low-level questions will limit exposure to and practice with high-level language that they need to develop. So, plan Raise the Bar questions to ask during read alouds. Afterward, provide High and Low Supports as necessary.

---

this student's personal experience to safe habitats for frogs (frogs are safer in a habitat that does not include cars). However, later the teacher chose not to follow up when a student initiated a conversation about going fishing after the text stated that frogs eat worms, because using worms as bait while fishing did not fit with the purpose of the read aloud or the learning objectives for the unit. Having a clear purpose helps us make better choices when guiding discussions during a read aloud.

When deciding how to introduce a text, consider (a) the learning objective, (b) the needs of the students in the class, and (c) the features of the text itself. First, consider the learning objectives and how to use the text to achieve that objective. Then, when introducing the text, describe the learning objective using child-friendly language (see the examples in Chapter 5).

Second, introduce the text in a way that meets the needs of the students in the class. Consider if students need some background information or visual supports to comprehend the text. For example, when reading *Tale of a Tadpole* (Wallace, 1998) with the learning objective of identifying the sequence of a frog's life cycle, one teacher chose to use props (miniature replicas of frog eggs, tadpole, froglet, and frog) to represent each stage. She showed students the props before reading the text and prepared students to put the props in sequence on a life cycle chart. Later, the teacher used the props to demonstrate the meaning of the word "camouflage" as well as to help students to understand a labeled illustration in the text. The props helped meet student needs while also generating interest and, therefore, they served as an excellent introduction to the text.

Third, we need to consider the text features of the book. Will students be familiar with the informational text features? Are there graphics that require instruction to interpret (e.g., a cross-sectional diagram)? Students may need a preview of some text features in order for the read aloud to be successful.

WRITE QUESTIONS AND COMMENTS

The next step is to plan several questions to ask or comments to make during the read aloud. Determine questions that will help students achieve the learning objectives and the purpose for each read aloud. Put them on sticky notes on the appropriate pages. Given the challenges of reading informational texts, these sticky notes help reduce our cognitive load during the read aloud. We can focus on reading the text with expression and helping students notice details in the illustrations (e.g., diagrams, charts) with confidence that our sticky notes will remind us of the questions and comments we intended to use.

What types of questions should teachers write? As discussed in Chapter 3, the answer is, questions that support language at low levels and high levels of cognitive thinking. When the purpose of the read aloud is to introduce students to a topic, write questions that focus on low levels of cognitive thinking. In order to extend students' thinking, also write questions that focus on high levels of cognitive thinking. Figure 3.3 provides ideas for Raise-the-Bar Strategies for informational texts. As suggested in Chapter 5, aim for roughly 60% of the questions to support low levels and 40% to support high levels of cognitive thinking. However, tailor that ratio given the needs of students, their familiarity with the topic, and how many times you have read a particular text. As students become more familiar with a particular text or topic, aim for greater proportions of high-level talk. Remember, students who are ELLs or who have disabilities also should be asked and expected to respond to questions requiring low and high levels of levels of cognitive thinking (for more ways to support these students, see Chapter 9).

SELECT ANCHOR CHARTS AND ACTIVITIES

Read alouds expose students to complex ideas and concepts. They also serve as a community-building activity that allows all students, regardless of their reading abilities, to share a common experience. Thus, a read aloud becomes a cornerstone for teaching and learning. To help students deal with complex texts and participate together for a common purpose, it is important to provide structure through activities that build and extend knowledge, visuals that support comprehension, and anchor charts that teach specific strategies students can apply now and in the future.

Therefore, this section includes activities and visuals to structure a read aloud. They are organized within the framework of the Reading Standards for Informational Text (i.e., Key Ideas and Details, Craft and Structure, Integration of Knowledge and Ideas), and the Language and Writing Standards. Our purpose for doing this is to reiterate that read alouds can be used to help students to achieve these expectations of the Common Core Standards. Although we did not include specific activities to support the Speaking and Listening Standards, those can be supported through all read alouds and all of these activities (see Chapter 5 for that discussion).

Activities to Target Key Ideas and Details

To achieve Key Ideas and Details of the Reading Standards for Informational Texts, students need to

- Ask and answer questions to demonstrate understanding of key details in a text
- Identify the main topic and retell details in increasingly more complex text
- Describe the relationship between two individuals, events, ideas, or bits of information (K–Grade 1)
- Describe the relations between historical events, scientific ideas or concepts, or steps in technical procedures (Grade 2)

We suggest the following two activities.

Key ideas and details anchor chart. As we read informational texts aloud, we want to help students identify the key idea of a passage and then to identify details that support that idea. To achieve this, we can use a key ideas and details anchor chart to help students organize and remember that information. A key ideas and details anchor chart could show, for example, a table (key idea) with legs (details), a pizza crust (key idea) with toppings (details), or an ice cream cone (key idea) with scoops of ice cream on top (details).

Regardless of the visual chosen, it can be used to support retelling or summarizing, both oral and in writing.

What's the Title? For this activity, do not show students the cover or title of the book. Tell students they will be listening to the text so that they can create a title and draw a picture for the cover of the book. Another option is to read a short section of a text and ask students to create a heading or subheading. Regardless of which option is chosen, this activity helps students practice identifying the main topic of a text or section of a text. Further, it can lend itself to interesting discussions as students present their titles and drawings and they realize that their peers may have slightly different ideas. Because there will be differences, students should justify their title and drawing based on information presented in the read aloud.

Activities to Target Craft and Structure

To achieve Craft and Structure standards for informational texts, students need to

- Ask and answer questions about unknown words (K), or determine or clarify the meaning of unknown words and phrases (Grades 1–2)
- Identify basic book concepts (K) and understand and use various text features to locate information (Grades 1–2)
- Name the author and illustrator and define their roles (K), distinguish between information provided by illustrations and text (Grade 1), and identify the main purpose of a text (Grade 2)

We suggest the following three activities.

Four Square Vocabulary anchor chart. This anchor chart helps students to clarify the meaning of words in a text (see Figure 6.1). It also facilitates deeper knowledge for target vocabulary that meets the Language Standards. Identify vocabulary that is important for comprehension and that may be unfamiliar to students. After reading the text, engage students in a discussion of the target words and complete the Four Square anchor chart. In addition to this anchor chart, the vocabulary connections anchor chart described in Chapter 5 also can be useful.

Text Features anchor chart. Informational texts contain specific features that students need to notice and use. However, these features can vary across texts. A text features anchor chart helps students to begin identifying these different features and to understand their purpose. See Figure 6.2 for a simplified text features anchor chart that can be used with young students. To

Figure 6.1. Example of a "Four Square Vocabulary" Anchor Chart

Illustration	Our Definition
	The natural environment of plants or animals

Habitat

Synonyms	Word Used in a Sentence
Home Environment	A bullfrog's habitat is a pond with lots of plants.

Figure 6.2. Example of a Simplified Text Features Anchor Chart

Text Features of Informational Texts

PURPOSES:

- Give Information
- Teach About a Topic

Visuals/Graphics Included

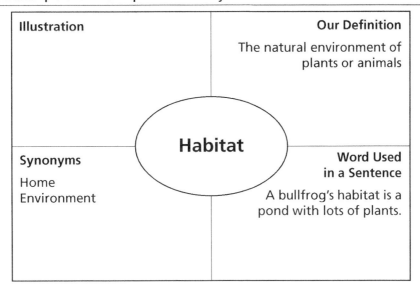

Table of Contents

Table of Contents

Chapter 1: Life of a Frog................2

Chapter 2: Where Frogs Live..........8

Chapter 3: What Frogs Eats...........12

Chapter 4: Frogs in Danger............16

Picture Glossary..........................20

Word Lists/Glossary

Picture Glossary

Frog Egg

Frog Eye

Webbed foot

Graphs/Tables

Gray Tree Frogs

Number of Frogs

1960 1980 2000 2020

Year

Headings

Where Frogs Live

Pictures with Captions

Maps and Diagrams

Where do frogs live in the United States? Everywhere!

In fact, over 100 species of frogs live in the United States.

use a text features anchor chart with older students, create a table in advance with headings such as What is it? What is its purpose? What does it look like? Identify text features in advance or ask students to locate features during a book walk. Add text features into the table and discuss their purpose and what they look like. In addition to identifying text features and their purpose, model how to use features such as headings, the table of contents, or the index to locate information, and explain the purpose of bold print, labels, and captions. One extension activity is a text features scavenger hunt in which students locate specific information within a text. For example, what is the definition of "froglet" and how did you locate your answer? Where would you look to learn information about frogs' defense mechanisms? What text features showed you where to look?

PIE anchor chart. Authors write texts for three primary reasons: (a) to persuade us of something (advertisements, billboards, speeches); (b) to inform us about a topic (nonfiction books, newspapers, magazines); or (c) to entertain us (stories, fables, folktales, poems). A PIE (persuade, inform, entertain) anchor chart illustrates these purposes and provides examples of texts that fit into each category (see Figure 6.3). While we do need to teach the concept of author's purpose as we read different genres, we do not need to discuss the author's purpose every time we read aloud.

Figure 6.3. Example of a PIE Anchor Chart

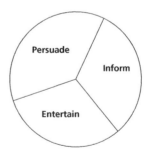

	Persuade	Inform	Entertain
Author is trying to:	Get us to do or think something	Teach or tell us about a topic	Help us have fun
I know because:	It has facts It has the author's opinions	It has facts	It has characters and actions I laugh or smile
Examples:	Commercials Advertisements Billboards Letter to someone in charge A public speech	Our science textbook Newspapers Magazines Recipes	*Knuffle Bunny* *Amazing Grace* Joke books Poetry

Hybrid texts are particularly useful when teaching students about an author's purpose because hybrid texts include both a story for entertainment purposes and information with the purpose of teaching about a topic (e.g., Magic School Bus series). For example, the following books contain multiple text purposes:

French, V., & Bartlett, A. (2000). *Growing Frogs*. Somerville, MA: Candlewick Press.

> Contains two separate lines of text, one story and one informational.

Greenburg, M. H. (1994). *Aunt Lilly's Laundromat*. New York, NY: Dutton Children's Books.

> Story about Aunt Lilly that also contains an informational sequence describing the process of sorting, washing, drying, and folding people's clothes.

Wright, M., & Kim, V. (2012). *Earth Day, Birthday!* Las Vegas, NV: Amazon Children's Publishing.

> A story about a monkey's birthday that includes information on ways to take care of the Earth as well as poetic features of rhyming and repeated verses.

Another way to create opportunities to discuss authors' purposes for writing is to create text sets that include different genres on the same topic. For example, in the Appendix, the unit on frogs includes a story, an informational text, and a poem.

Activities to Target Integration of Knowledge and Ideas

To achieve Integration of Knowledge and Ideas for the informational text standards, students need to

- Describe the connection between illustrations and details (K), use illustrations and details to describe key ideas (Grade 1), and explain how images add to and clarify meaning (Grade 2)
- Identify the reasons an author gives to support key points (K–Grade 1) and describe how the reasons support those points (Grade 2)
- Identify similarities and differences between two texts on the same topic (K–Grade 1) and compare and contrast the key points in two texts on the same topic (Grade 2)

We can implement the following three activities to help students develop higher levels of cognitive thinking needed to achieve the standards of integration of knowledge and ideas.

Anchor charts: Graphs, tables, and timelines. Students need to learn how to interpret and use the information contained in illustrations in informational texts. These illustrations often include graphics that organize information for the reader, and they often require that we read from bottom to top, from right to left, or in a circular or zigzag fashion. Three such graphic organizers are graphs, tables, and timelines. Graphs, such as pie graphs, line graphs, and bar graphs, are intended to illustrate the relationships among different variables. We might need to read them from bottom to top or in a circular fashion. Tables contain columns and rows that are typically labeled and that give information about the topic. It helps to read the labels for the columns and rows first, and then to read the content in the table. A timeline shows events over a certain time period through the use of dates and pictures and words. Reading timelines requires finding where to start and then following the direction of the arrows.

Creating graphics as a class is one way for students to understand these illustrations. For example, during a study of weather, students could identify their favorite season and then the class could create a bar graph or a pie chart to illustrate those preferences. To teach a more complex graphic, record the temperature each day to create a line graph (e.g., days on the *x*-axis, temperature in degrees Fahrenheit on the *y*-axis) and model reading the labels for each axis first and then moving up to read the information inside portrayed by the line.

Graphics also can be used to organize the content in informational texts. For example, while studying the ecosystem, 2nd-grade students could create a diagram showing a food chain after reading aloud *What Are Food Chains and Food Webs* (Kalman & Langille, 2005). When learning about life cycles, a timeline could be used to observe and document how a caterpillar builds a chrysalis and eventually becomes a butterfly, including the sequence of steps and their durations. Likewise, as students learn about their own families or local community during social studies, they can work together to create a timeline with dates, facts, and images of important events that have occurred. We recommend Moline's (2011) text on visual literacy as a highly accessible and engaging resource for ideas on teaching and using graphics in the classroom.

Web diagrams or concept maps. Web diagrams or concept maps are a type of graphic organizer useful for showing concepts plus the relationships between them (Birbili, 2006). Concepts are written in boxes or circles and then the relationships between them are represented with lines and arrows. Creating a concept map helps students to organize the ideas from a text read aloud and its illustrations, and it can support their explanations of complex information. For example, in the Appendix unit on frogs, the students helped generate answers to the question "What do frogs need to live and grow?" As students worked to answer the question, the teacher put the ideas onto a concept map (see Figure 6.4). Then the concept map supported students as they explained the answer to the original question. Students were able to form much more complete answers when they used the concept map as a visual support. So the visual support helped both to facilitate Integration of Knowledge and Ideas and to achieve the Language and Speaking standards.

Agree/Disagree. Engaging students in an Agree/Disagree activity (Harvey & Goudvis, 2007) helps them understand reasons why an author includes information in a text. Make a list of details that support the main idea in the text you will be reading aloud, as well as details that do not support the main idea or do not belong. For example, in reading a text about frogs, some details supporting the main idea are "Some frogs hibernate in the winter" and "Some frogs use camouflage as a defense mechanism." Details that would not support the main idea might include "All frogs are green" or "Kermit the Frog is a famous frog." As you read these details, ask students to agree or disagree, with a thumbs-up or thumbs-down, if they think the author would include the

Figure 6.4. Example Concept Map: "What Do Frogs Need to Live and Grow?"

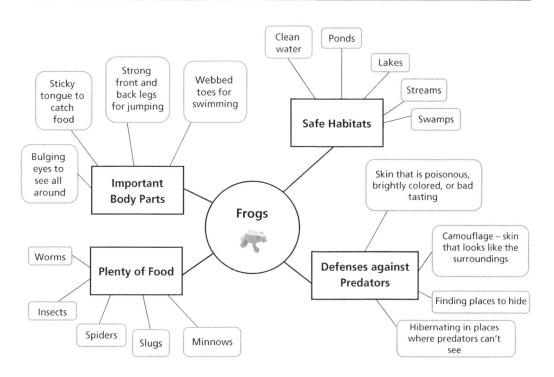

information in the text or not. Ask students to support their decision based on a reason and evidence from the text.

Activities to Target Language Standards

Talk related to informational text read alouds allows students to engage in respectful conversations, express their ideas clearly using conventions of Standard English grammar, and learn and use sophisticated vocabulary from the text. The following two activities support these language standards.

Concept sorts. A concept sort helps students learn vocabulary and understand the relationships between words and ideas. Create a set of word cards related to a topic and, if needed, include pictures. Ask students to sort words prior to a read aloud to determine what they know about the topic or after a read aloud to encourage students to think deeply about the words and concepts. To support students, have them do a "closed sort" by placing word cards under predetermined categories and explain their reason for placing those words under each category. Or conduct an "open sort" by asking students to sort the word cards into their own categories and explain their reasons for various groupings. Figure 6.5 shows how word cards related to vocabulary might be sorted under predetermined categories; however, students often come up with other solutions that make sense after they explain their reasoning. So it's good practice to always listen to their rationales before deciding on how to support them!

Figure 6.5. Example Concept Sort: Weather Words

Precipitation		Temperature	Wind	Severe Weather
Mist	Flurries	Wind chill	Breeze	Tornado
Fog	Sleet	Heat index	Blustery	Hurricane
Rain	Hail	Hot	Gust	Flood
Snow		Cold	Gale	Blizzard

Props or prop boxes. As with literature, props create interest in an informational text read aloud, and prop boxes can be used extend the learning. For example, we observed one teacher who dressed up in a bat costume to introduce the book *Bats* (Gibbons, 1999) and later related the parts of her costume to the surface diagram of a bat included in the book. Another teacher used a flashlight and different-shaped objects to show how a light source casts shadows and how changes in the location of the light source affected the size and shape of the shadows created.

Taking props one step further, a prop box for role-playing supports learning. For example, when the class is studying plants, a gardener prop box could include gardening tools, gloves, a watering can, seed packets, artificial flowers, plastic fruits and vegetables, a length of old hose, a spray nozzle, gardening hats, and baskets to collect flowers or vegetables. During play using the props, students use vocabulary and engage in dialogue that is appropriate to the topic. Props can be used with more challenging tasks, too. For example, 2nd-graders could use props to create a map to design their garden, or they could examine plants under a magnifying glass and then draw and label the parts in a science journal.

Activities to Target Writing

Read alouds can become a springboard for drawing, dictating, and writing. As students learn about a topic, they can participate in shared or independent research projects that also allow them to strengthen their writing skills. Further, students can use a variety of digital tools to investigate their topic and demonstrate their learning (see Chapter 8). The following two activities support these writing standards.

Writing a summary. Identifying key ideas and details is the first step in learning to summarize, an important comprehension strategy. Activities previously described provide a framework for helping students to summarize (e.g., key ideas and details anchor chart) and to use more technical vocabulary in their summary (e.g., four square and concept sorts). Use those to help students identify the information to include in a summary. Then encourage students to wrap up their summary by writing something interesting that they learned or by asking a provocative question. Sentence starters are helpful:

- Did you know that . . . ?
- I learned that . . .
- It was interesting to find out that . . .
- Another important fact about . . .
- I still wonder . . .

Sentence frames also support summarizing (Marzano, Pickering, & Pollock, 2001). When providing a sentence frame, be sure it aligns with the text structure of the reading.

- *Description:* A _____ is a kind of _____that _____.
- *Sequence:* First, _____, then _____, and finally _____.
- *Problem/Solution:* _____ needs _____ but _____ so _____.
- *Compare and Contrast:* _____ and _____ are similar because _____. However, they are also different because _____, while _____.

An example of a problem/solution sentence frame related to what frogs need to live and grow would be "Frogs need clean water to live but pollution is making the water too dirty for frogs to live in so we need to prevent chemicals and pollution from getting into the water."

Writing for various purposes. Encourage students to use knowledge gained from informational text read alouds to inform, persuade, or entertain others. For example, if studying the Amazon River and forest, students could

- Describe a day in the life of indigenous people of the Amazon.
- Create a facts sheet about different animals of the rain forest.
- Write a travel brochure describing a boat trip down the Amazon River.
- Explain deforestation and persuade people to be more environmentally conscious.
- Write an entertaining narrative set in the rain forest.

Before writing, students can engage in shared research by watching videos, visiting educational websites, or talking with local experts. Also, depending on the purpose, students can add graphs, tables, timelines, maps, drawings, or photographs. See Chapter 8 for ideas on using digital resources for these types of writing activities.

SUMMARY

In this chapter, we considered the benefits and challenges of informational text read alouds and described ways to plan for a read aloud in order to mini- mize the challenges and maximize learning. We described various ways to use informational texts, activities, and anchor charts to help students achieve the Common Core Standards. Although informational text read alouds typically support learning of content information, we always strive to make read alouds fun and engaging, regardless of the genre. As we increase the frequency of using informational texts for read alouds, we see how much fun they can be.

CHAPTER 7

Poetry

> Truly fine poetry must be read aloud. A good poem does not allow itself to be read in a low voice or silently. If we can read it silently, it is not a valid poem: a poem demands pronunciation. Poetry always remembers that it was an oral art before it was a written art. It remembers that it was first song.
>
> —Jorge Luis Borges, *Seven Nights*

Engaging in the arts, such as poetry, allows students to develop an appreciation for the beauty around them. Poetry inspires wonder, awe, curiosity, and personal connections. Developmentally, the arts provide students with other benefits. For example, drawing and painting help students develop fine motor skills that are important for writing and keyboarding; sculpting with clay helps students develop visual-spatial skills important for interpreting pictures of three-dimensional objects from digital media and books; dramatization helps students develop verbal and nonverbal communication skills; music helps students develop coordination, auditory and spatial skills, and reasoning abilities.

Despite these benefits, the art we expose students to is often determined by our own experience and comfort level. For example, some teachers might prefer music and movement, while other teachers prefer visual arts such as drawing, painting, and sculpture. While we should encourage students to engage in variety of art activities, the Common Core State Standards expect us to teach a particular form of art—that is, poetry. However, a word of caution: Poetry first and foremost is art and it should be savored. Only after enjoying the aesthetic aspects of a poem should we begin to analyze it. Dissecting a poem without enjoying it defeats the purpose of poetry!

BENEFITS AND CHALLENGES OF READING POETRY ALOUD

Reading poetry aloud provides many benefits to students. Poetry contains "rich, precise, imaginative language" that students can think about and discuss (Heard, 2012, p. 8). Rich and sophisticated vocabulary helps teach about synonyms and the nuances of word choices. The language in poetry creates opportunities to introduce the concept of literal and nonliteral language and to explore figurative language (similes, metaphor, idioms, personification, alliteration, onomatopoeia). Poetry demonstrates how words and phrases evoke feelings and appeal to our senses of seeing, hearing, feeling, tasting, and smelling. Further, focusing on the content of poems teaches students to think about common objects and events in different or unique ways. Finally, because poems are often written in a concise manner, they can be read several times during a read aloud. This creates opportunities for students both to enjoy the magic in the poem and to discuss its content and form more deeply.

On the other hand, reading poetry aloud can be challenging, for a variety of reasons. Challenges include dealing with our own fears about poetry, explaining sophisticated vocabulary and figurative language, and balancing the focus between poetry as an art form versus an instructional tool. Let's discuss these challenges.

First, our own limited exposure to poetry may cause fears that make us hesitant to use poetry in the classroom. We may have stage fright, knowing that reading a poem aloud is like a performance. We may fear that we lack the skills to interpret poetry ourselves and use it as a tool for instruction. We may fear that the poem will touch upon difficult emotions and we won't know how to respond in the discussion that follows. Careful selection of poems in the planning process can help alleviate these fears.

Second, poetry can be difficult because of the vocabulary, figurative language, and grammar (Elster & Hanauer, 2002). For example, if a poem contains too many unusual words or too much figurative language, students may have difficulty understanding it. Likewise, poetry often involves different syntactic patterns and, therefore, can be challenging for students. However, multiple readings along with discussion of a poem can help students understand the language, especially with teacher scaffolding.

Finally, another challenge is that the aesthetic value of poetry can get lost when we use poetry for instructional purposes. We have to work on achieving a balance! Focusing on a poem first as a piece of artwork, and later turning our focus to its instructional value, will help us to achieve this balance. That is, we must refrain from just dissecting poems or using poetry simply as a tool to teach decoding or comprehension skills.

Although there are challenges when integrating poetry into read alouds, the benefits are worth it. Also, challenges can be overcome through good planning and learning to apply the responsive-interactive strategies during the read aloud. Planning ahead is the best way to help us feel comfortable reading poetry aloud. As with other genres, planning does not need to be time-consuming. However, we advocate a sequence of steps that is a bit different from the sequence we recommended for literature and informational texts. The goal is to help us feel more comfortable and confident with this genre. Thus, planning includes these five steps:

1. Choose a poem.
2. Identify the learning objective(s).
3. Plan a method for introducing the poem.
4. Write questions and comments to use.
5. Select anchor charts and activities.

CHOOSE A POEM

Rather than identifying learning objectives first, as we suggested with literature and informational texts, we recommend choosing a poem first. Consider poems that students will be able to relate to and that they will enjoy. This might be a classic Mother Goose nursery rhyme, a humorous poem written by a children's poet such as Mary Ann Hoberman or Jack Prelutsky, or even a poem from the literary canon and written by poets such as Maya Angelou or Langston Hughes. Also, consider poems that you enjoy so that the poem will come alive when you read it, which is important for conveying appreciation of poetry.

In the process of choosing a poem, read it aloud several times. What is the aesthetic value? Does the poem inspire a particular emotion or sensation? Does it create an image? Does the poem spark an idea or make you wonder? Identify the aesthetic feature that you want to focus on during the read aloud. When reading poetry aloud, we want to focus on its aesthetic value before its academic learning. Next, read the poem aloud to consider its potential academic purposes. How can it be used to achieve learning objectives?

In addition to looking through books of poetry to choose a poem, consider digital resources. Listening to a poem read aloud by the author or a performer is a wonderful experience. Also, listening to other voices with different pitch and intonation is engaging and provides other models of reading fluency that are important for beginning readers. Some sites (e.g., www.poetryfoundation. org/children/; www.poets.org/poetsorg/text/poems-kids) include images and animation along with the reading. Further, some books of poetry include a CD of the poems being read aloud, as in *Hip Hop Speaks to Children* (Giovanni, 2008) and *The Carnival of the Animals* (Prelutsky, Saint-Saens, & GrandPre, 2010).

A poem, like a narrative or informational text, can be a "stand-alone" read aloud or it can be integrated into a unit. That is, we can read a poem just for the sake of reading that poem. If reading poetry is not part of your existing routine, it might be easier to choose a poem to read without worrying about integrating it into a unit. However, think about how poetry can be part of your regular routine. For example, you might start each class day by sharing a poem or have a Poetry Café every Friday (described later in the chapter). Poetry also can be integrated into a unit of study. For example, for science, you might consider poems in *National Geographic Book of Animal Poetry: 200 Poems with Photographs That Squeak, Soar, and Roar!* (Lewis, 2012).

When learning about different cultures in social studies, consider ¡Pío Peep!: *Traditional Spanish Nursery Rhymes* (Ada & Campoy, 2003) or *Jaha and Jamil Went Down the Hill: An African Mother Goose* (Kroll & Roundtree, 1995). There are even poems for math, such as *Marvelous Math: A Book of Poems* (Hopkins & Barbour, 2001). Poems can be used to achieve the existing learning objectives for the unit, but they also likely provide opportunities to address additional learning objectives.

IDENTIFY THE LEARNING OBJECTIVE(S)

Once you have chosen a poem, it is time to determine learning objectives. Remember, however, our first objective is for students to appreciate the art and beauty of the poem. Thus, first help students experience the poem aesthetically. Second, we can identify a learning objective. Can we focus on some aspect of the form (e.g., phonological awareness, text structure, punctuation, grammar)? For example, does the poem include rhymes or alliteration to foster phonological awareness? Could the poem support oral and reading fluency? Does it include a refrain, or is it a poem written for two voices? Can we focus on content (vocabulary, concepts, figurative language, how the words convey feelings)? Does the poem conjure up silly images and ideas? Does it evoke emotions or stimulate the senses? Although there may be many possible learning objectives for any specific poem, choose only one or two to highlight and discuss. Trying to accomplish too much will kill the poem!

PLAN A METHOD FOR INTRODUCING THE POEM

Introducing a poem is different from introducing literature or informational texts. In previous chapters, we have talked about the importance of making students aware of the purpose of the read aloud. In the case of poetry, we want to focus on the aesthetic value of the poem first and not mention our academic purposes for reading the poem. We do this for good reasons.

Initially, we always want students to experience the poem as art; telling students an academic purpose can interfere with experiencing the poem. For example, if we tell students before reading the poem that we will be talking about the verbs, or words that convey action, in the poem, then students might listen primarily for those words rather than experiencing the art of the poem. They immediately start analyzing the poem in an academic way, and that ruins the aesthetic experience of it.

Therefore, our initial introduction of a poem needs to focus on aesthetics. For example, when reading a poem about winter, we could show students beautiful photographs of snow-covered trees or mountains, icicles, snowmen, or close-ups of snowflakes. Or we could start by showing a snow globe, shaking it and silently watching as the little flakes fall to the bottom. We prime the pump, so to speak, and then we read the poem aloud with expression. After discussing the experience of the poem, the aesthetics, we can move on to our academic purposes for reading it.

At that point, we can mark the shift from aesthetics to our academic purposes by explaining that now that we have experienced the poem as the author wanted us to, we will read the poem again for a different purpose. For example, for one of the text sets in the Appendix, we used the poem "The Polliwogs" initially to help students to visualize and use their imaginations to see, hear, smell, and feel the tadpoles. We listened to appreciate the rhymes and rhythms. After savoring the poem that way, we read it again in order to achieve the academic purposes of noticing (a) the words (*quiver*, *shiver*, *jiggle*, and *jog*) the author used to describe the movements of the tadpoles and (b) the text features (uneven print) the author used to make the words look like they were moving like tadpoles on the page! While listening to the poem again, we used discussion to achieve these academic purposes.

Finally, as you prepare to read a poem aloud, practice reading the poem with expression, and consider ways to get students participating that may differ from literature or informational texts (see Box 7.1).

WRITE QUESTIONS AND COMMENTS

As with the other genres, write specific questions and comments that encourage students to think more deeply about the poem. But remember, we have two types of purposes for reading poetry, an aesthetic purpose and an academic purpose, and we need questions for each of these.

For aesthetic purposes, our goal is to be open-ended and nondirective. We need to carefully plan the prompts that open up the discussion, such as "Tell me about the poem" or "Talk to me about this poem." Other open-ended questions include

- Close your eyes. What do you see as I read this poem?
- As I read, what does this poem remind you of?
- How did that poem make you feel?
- What did you notice about this poem?
- What did you like about this poem? What did you dislike about this poem?

For our academic purposes, we can write questions that help students achieve the learning objectives. Some questions should require low levels of cognitive thinking, and others should Raise the Bar. For example, for the

---

BOX 7.1. ADDITIONAL SUGGESTIONS FOR POETRY READ ALOUDS

There are other considerations and opportunities when reading poetry aloud compared with literature or informational text read aloud. Here are some additional suggestions as you plan, read, and reread poetry.

➤ **Read expressively—consider the following:**
  - Slow down or speed up to alter your rate.
  - Emphasize the rhyme or beat.
  - Use a melodious voice.
  - Stress and elongate words.
  - Vary your volume, read part of the poem loudly or quietly.

➤ **Encourage students to**
  - Participate through reading along, acting out, gesturing, clapping, and chiming.
  - Read portions of the poem, such as the repeated lines, or include several voices reading the poem.
  - Read along to increase fluency and to practice using the features of expression you have modeled (e.g., slowing down, speeding up, stressing words, varying volume).

➤ **Record the read aloud and listen to it multiple times; record students reading the poem.**

➤ **End the read aloud session by rereading the poem one last time without interruption.**

➤ **Invite guests to your class to read a favorite poem.**

---

poem "The Spring Peepers" (in Florian, 2001), about small frogs that begin croaking in the spring, we asked the following Raise the Bar questions:

- Think about the video we watched of spring peeper frogs. What did they look like when they were making their call? What words did the author of this poem use to describe that?
- In this poem, it is the sound of the spring peepers that is keeping the man in the illustration awake. When have you been kept awake by some kind of noise? What noise was it? How did it make you feel?

These questions were the foundation for our discussion and helped focus the talk on our learning objectives. They also helped us to relate the contents of the poem to digital sources and informational texts we had used earlier in the unit. As students answered these questions, we responded to their contributions using the responsive-interactive strategies.

One issue remains as we plan questions and comments to use: When do we present them? Unlike other genres, where it is possible to stop and ask questions or make comments during reading, it is best to read a poem in its entirety and ask our questions afterward. Since poems tend to be short, at least those for students in the preschool-to-2nd-grade range, we can often read a poem aloud several times before we begin to talk about specific lines or aspects of the poem.

SELECT ANCHOR CHARTS AND ACTIVITIES

Anchor charts and activities provide support for students during a read aloud of poetry. In fact, because students may have less exposure to poetry compared with other text genres, they may benefit even more from such support. The following anchor charts and activities provide scaffolding that can improve students' ability to contribute verbally and learn from the read aloud. In addition to supporting students, they help us stay focused on the objective and provide structure for explaining concepts. The anchor charts and activities in the following sections support the Common Core State Standards.

Activities to Target Key Ideas and Details

Poetry can be used to help students ask and answer questions about key details, retell the central message or lesson, or describe characters and setting or main topic and details. Here are two activities to help achieve these standards.

Poetry suitcase. As with as other genres, props help poetry come alive, heighten curiosity, or make a poem more concrete for students. In fact, Janet Wong (www.poetrysuitcase.com/) recommends creating a "poetry suitcase" filled with props. There are many ways to create a poetry suitcase. One method is to choose poems related to a particular topic and fill a poetry suitcase with objects related to that topic. Students can discuss which object best represents the key idea in a poem and which objects represent details. For "The Spring Peepers" (in Florian, 2001), a wood percussion frog instrument could represent the key idea of poem—that spring peepers are noisy—while plastic flowers could represent spring and a small pillow could represent the lack of sleep some people experience because of the noisy spring peepers. Another method for creating a poetry suitcase is to choose a variety of poems students like and objects that relate to each poem. Students can choose an object and then explain why that object best represents a poem, which requires that they focus on key ideas. Considering Mother Goose nursery rhymes, a stuffed sheep could represent "Little Bo Peep," a plastic egg could represent "Humpty Dumpty," and a rubber spider could represent "Little Miss Muffet."

Such objects can inspire discussion of the characters in the poems. A poetry suitcase is an exciting way to read several poems aloud during one sitting, and to get students thinking and talking about them.

Drawing a poem. Poetry often evokes strong images or feelings, which are essentially the key ideas. So rather than showing students the images that accompany a poem, ask students to draw their own images. Read a poem several times slowly so that students can add more detail with each reading. Afterward, ask students to share their drawings and explain what words or phrases encouraged them to draw particular details. For poems that evoke strong feelings or emotions, you might notice that students are using certain colors or certain types of lines or shapes. Ask them to explain their reasons for those choices.

Activities to Target Craft and Structure

Poetry provides many opportunities to teach vocabulary, discuss words that convey feelings or appeal to the senses, and notice how phrases contribute to the rhythm. Different types of poems can be compared to understand structure, and poems can be compared with other genres. Here are two activities to help foster knowledge of the craft and structure of poetry.

Using visualization or imagery. Using visualization or creating images involves using all our senses. We can see it, hear it, taste it, smell it, and feel it (tactile and emotional), and this helps us gain a deeper understanding of the text and recall key ideas and details (Gambrell & Jawitz, 1993). Poets use words and phrases in purposeful ways to appeal to various senses. Before reading a poem, help students think about their senses by describing sensations. For example, if reading Robert Louis Stevenson's poem "The Swing" (www.poetryfoundation.org/poem/171919), you might ask: What does swinging remind you of? What do you see and hear when you are swinging? How do you feel when you swing really high? Helpful sentence starters for visualizing include

- I'm picturing . . .
- I can imagine . . .
- I can feel . . .
- I can see . . .
- I can taste . . .
- I can touch . . .
- I can hear . . .

Once students have thought about how experiences can create different sensations and have practiced using words to describe those sensations, they are ready to use imagery while listening to a poem. Encourage students to think about how the poem engages their senses and discuss what words and phrases helped to inspire those images.

To extend this activity, create a poet's words anchor chart to engage students in discussions about the words a poet used to create those images and sensations (see Figure 7.1 for an example). Write down students' thoughts and the poet's words and phrases that inspired those thoughts. The vocabulary connections and figurative language anchor charts described in Chapter 5 also can be used to target word knowledge during poetry read alouds.

Poetry type anchor chart. A poetry type anchor chart makes explicit the features of each type of poem we choose to target and read aloud. For example, we could create an anchor chart that compares features of four common types of poems (e.g., free verse, lyrical, narrative, and humorous) or one that visually illustrates four specific types of poems (e.g., acrostic, concrete or shape, haiku, limerick). Similarly, an anchor chart can be used to make comparisons across and within genres. For example, students could compare the poem "Frog Serenade" (in Heard & Dewey, 1992) to the informational text *Frogs! Amazing Amphibians* (Editors of *Time for Kids* & Satterfield, 2006), or they could compare a version of the story of Cinderella to Ann Hoberman's poem by the same title found in *You Read to Me, I'll Read to You: Very Short Fairy Tales to Read Together* (Hoberman & Emberley, 2012).

Activities to Target Integration of Knowledge and Ideas

Poetry can help students understand connections between text and the illustrations and to use text features or illustrations to support their understanding of the poem's content. Poetry also helps students to think about a topic in unique ways to build knowledge or to consider a poet's approach to a topic. Here are two activities to help achieve these standards.

Poetry and art. Poetry and art are naturally connected. In fact, there are many books of poems that include beautiful artwork such as Douglas Florian's *Mammaliabilia* (2004) and Eric Carle's *Animals, Animals* (1989). Further, there are several books inspired by art such as *Heart to Heart: New Poems Inspired by Twentieth-Century American Art* (Greenburg, 2001), or *Paint Me a Poem: Poems Inspired by Masterpieces of Art* (Rowden, 2005). Poetry that includes artwork provides an excellent context for discussing the relationships between the illustrations and the text. What does the artwork add to our understanding of the text of the poem? How does the artwork support the words in conveying feelings or appealing to the senses? Finally, art can be used to inspire students to write poetry, just as poetry can be used to inspire students to create art. This also supports the Speaking and Listening Standard of adding images to descriptions to clarify ideas, thoughts, and feelings.

Figure 7.1. Example of a Poet's Words Anchor Chart

For: Hollingsworth, S. (2015). "Pitter Patter, Pitter Pat." Unpublished poem.

Pitter patter, pitter pat
At my window, "what is that?"
Rain drops dancing on the sill.
I am quiet. I am still.

Listening to water's rhythm,
Suddenly my toes are tapping.
Now my body can't stay still!
Arms are waving. Hands are clapping!

Quickly as my feet will carry,
I throw on my boots and hat.
Stop to listen for that rhythm:
Pitter patter, pitter pat.

"Mom, can I go out and play?
This rainy music calls to me!"
Mom says "yes", I'm on my way!
Dancing, splashing, spinning, wheeee!

Soon my socks are sopping wet.
Soon my cheeks are red and chilly.
I don't mind; my heart is warm.
I'm dancing, running, being silly.

Then, once more, I'm very still,
Listening for drips and drops.
But it's quiet all around,
The sun is out. The rain has stopped.

Now I feel the warmth of sunshine.
Now I'm quiet. Now I listen.
Sunshine makes the birds start singing,
Makes the puddles shine and glisten.

What a day! My heart is happy!
Rain and sun and cold and warm!
There is music all around us,
Even in the darkest storm.

Reflecting with poems. Poetry encourages deep thinking and reflection—just consider Robert Frost's *The Road Less Traveled* or Maya Angelou's *I Know Why the Caged Bird Sings*. But how can we help young students use poetry to engage in cognitively challenging thinking? One way is to ask students to compare and contrast how illustrators interpret the same poem; for example, consider Jan Brett (Lear & Brett, 1996), James Marshall (Lear & Marshall, 1998), and Anne Mortimer's (Lear & Mortimer, 2006) illustrations of Edward Lear's *The Owl and the Pussycat*. Another way we can help students to think more deeply is to show them how poetry helps us to think about common objects and events in different ways and from different perspectives. For example, Robert Louis Stevenson's poem "My Shadow" (www.poetryfoundation.org/poem/171951) will encourage students to think more deeply about their own shadows. In addition, the making inferences and making connections anchor charts described in Chapter 5 are also useful for helping students integrate knowledge and ideas during poetry read alouds (see example in Figure 7.2).

Activities to Target Writing

As discussed in previous chapters, read alouds can become a springboard for writing activities. Writing poetry can be particularly motivating because students can be creative with a topic, word choices, grammar, and the structure of their poem, and poems tend to be short!

Figure 7.1. Example of a Poet's Words Anchor Chart (continued)

Sense	Our Thoughts	The Poet's Words
See	A child putting on her boots and raincoat.	Quickly as my feet will carry,
		I throw on my boots and hat.
	A child dancing outside in the rain with her arms waving and clapping, body spinning, feet stomping in puddles.	Arms are waving. Hands are clapping!
		Dancing, splashing, spinning, wheeee!
		I'm dancing, running, being silly.
	Then the child stops and is still.	Then, once more, I'm very still
	After the rain, the sun shines in the puddles.	Sunshine makes the birds start singing,
		Makes the puddles shine and glisten.
Hear	The raindrops on the window and roof	Pitter patter, pitter pat
		At my window, "what is that?"
	Child clapping her hands	Arms are waving. Hands are clapping.
	Quiet	Then, once more, I'm very still,
	Drips and drops of water	Now I'm quiet. Now I listen.
	Birds singing	But it's quiet all around,
	The rain makes its own kind of music	Listening for drips and drops.
		Sunshine makes the birds start singing
		There is music all around us, even in the darkest storm.
Smell	Wet dirt	(no words from the poet but the poem made us think this)
	How the air smells when it rains	
Taste	Taste rain in my mouth dripping down from my cheeks	(no words from the poet but the poem made us think this)
Touch/ Movement	Tapping my foot on the floor	Suddenly my toes are tapping.
	Cold and wet on my cheeks	Soon my cheeks are red and chilly.
	Wet feet inside my boots	Soon my socks are sopping wet.
	Warm sun on my face	Now I feel the warmth of sunshine.
		Rain and sun and cold and warm!
Emotion	Excitement	This rainy music calls to me!
	Silly	I'm dancing, running, being silly.
	Happiness, calm	Dancing, splashing, spinning, wheeee!
		I don't mind; my heart is warm.
		What a day! My heart is happy!

Poetry walk. To encourage poetry writing, take students on a nature walk. Prepare for the walk by talking about what they might notice or focus on, such as trees, flowers, birds, insects, shadows, textures, colors, or smells. While on the walk, encourage students to use all their senses to notice the world around them. For example, what colors and shapes are the leaves? What do they

Figure 7.2. Example of a Making Connections Anchor Chart

For: Stevenson, R. L. (1947). "My Shadow." Available at www.poetryfoundation.org/poem/171951	
Text-to-Self	When it said "he likes to grow" it reminded me of how I can make a shadow and can change its size and shape.
	My shadow is like the shadow in the poem because I see it on the playground when I'm playing.
Text-to-Text	The poem reminds me of *Bear Shadow* (Asch, 1990).
	The poem reminds me of *What Makes a Shadow* (Bulla & Otani, 1994).
Text-to-Media	Sid the Kid and his friends saw their shadow on the playground and they learned about shadows (pbskids.org/video/?guid=c7ddd324-a8fb-4745-9c77-6479f11bd678)

hear—birds chirping or bees buzzing? What do they smell—freshly cut grass or smoke from burning leaves? With respect to touch, you could ask if all tree trunks have the same texture or what the temperature is outside. Of course, if your school is located in a city or neighborhood, you might have them notice the shapes and colors of doors or windows, the sounds of vehicles, the textures of buildings or the sidewalk, the images created by light and shadows, or the smells of a bakery or restaurant. Encourage students to take notes or draw pictures to help them remember what they notice. After the walk, help students to organize their thoughts and consider words and phrases that capture sensations and emotions. The nature walk, their notes, and the words and phrases generated can be used to write their own poems about the experience.

Poet's toolbox anchor chart. Poets use many literary or poetic devices and a poet's toolbox anchor chart helps students to learn about and use them in their own writing. This anchor chart can consist of one column for tools (e.g., alliteration, hyperbole, metaphor, onomatopoeia, personification, repetition, and simile) and another column for the definition, an example, or both (see Figure 7.3). As you read poems, refer to the chart to help students notice the devices a poet used and add new devices as you encounter and teach them.

Activities to Target Foundational Skills

Although all genres can be used to address foundational skills (e.g., print concepts, phonological awareness, and phonics and word recognition), we focus on them only in the context of poetry. This is in part because poetry provides rich opportunities to address these standards but also because we prefer to use other genres to facilitate rich discussions about content and language, rather than distracting students with a print focus. Here are three activities to help achieve foundational skills standards using poetry.

Figure 7.3. Example of a Poet's Toolbox Anchor Chart

Poet's Tools	Definition	Example
Rhyme	Endings of words sound the same	Jill/hill; moon/spoon; rose/nose
Alliteration	Same sound at the beginning of words	Billions of bursting bubbles in the bathtub
Simile	Comparison using "like" or "as"	Quick like a fox; slow as a snail
Onomatopoeia	Words that imitate sounds or the actions they describe	buzz, pow, slurp, squish
Personification	When animals or objects take on human traits	The leaves danced with the wind.
Hyperbole	Exaggeration	I'm so hungry I could eat a horse!

Mini-lesson on print concepts. Shape or concrete poems are a wonderful way to help students to understand print concepts. In these poems, the text creates a picture or outline representing the topic of the poem. For example, in the poem "Giraffe" from *Doodle Dandies: Poems That Take Shape* (Lewis & Desimini, 2002), the text is presented in the shape of a giraffe. No doubt there will be interesting conversations about text, conversations that can then be used to teach students about writing conventions (e.g., capitalization, punctuation) and the use of different font styles (e.g., bold, italics, capitalization) to convey meaning. Two books with shape or concrete poems are

Graham, J. B., & Davis, N. (2003). *Flicker Flash*. Boston, MA: Houghton Mifflin
Graham, J. B., & Scott, S. (2001). *Splish Splash*. Boston, MA: Houghton Mifflin

Mini-lessons on rhyme and rhythm. Rhyme and rhythm provide a framework to a poem and bring a sense of balance or harmony. Rhythm and rhyme can also help a reader to predict what is coming next in a poem. After reading a poem with rhymes, point out or encourage students to notice the rhyming words and discuss how rhymes can create rhythm. Also, help students understand and use rhyme by creating a set of rhyming picture or word cards. Ask students to match pictures or words that rhyme and encourage them to generate other rhymes, real or nonsense. To help students notice the rhythm of a poem (also an element of craft and structure), consider using musical instruments. For example, a student might quickly shake a maraca as you read "Hummingbird" from *Creatures of Earth, Sea, and Sky* (Heard & Dewey, 1992) or slowly rub fluted rhythm sticks together to simulate frogs croaking when listening to "The Bullfrog" from *Lizards, Frogs, and Polliwogs* (Florian, 2001). Students can tap out the beat in a poem by using drums, and they can create different moods by changing the rhythms, the intensity, and the speed of their beats on the drums. Poetry that is sung or chanted or that has musical accompaniment, such as some of the poems included in *Hip Hop Speaks to Children* (Giovanni, 2008), can help students understand these concepts.

Mini-lessons on repetition of words, phrases, and sounds. Repetition is a tool that poets use to create rhythm, emphasize a feeling or an idea, or create a sense of unity. Show how repetition of a word creates unity, as well as emphasizes a point, by reading aloud a poem such as "Pigs" from *Animal Tracks: Wild Poems to Read Aloud* (Ghigna & Speirs, 2004), in which every line begins with the word *pig*. Or read the poem "Snow" from *The Llama Who Had No Pajama* (Hoberman & Fraser, 2006), which repeats the word *snow* and the phrase "snow on the sidewalk" to emphasize just how much snow there is and that it is everywhere!

Alliteration, the repetition of the same sound at the beginning of words, brings attention to words and helps to create an overall feeling. Read a poem such as "Balloons" (in Hoberman & Fraser, 2006) and ask students what sound (/b/) is repeated and why the poet may have repeated that particular sound. If students are unsure of why the poet chose a sound, have them repeat the sound many times. In the case of "Balloon," we're sure it will remind them of the anticipation they feel before a balloon bursts.

Poetry Café. The Poetry Café creates an opportunity for students to read their favorite poem aloud. While students can choose to read "live," others may prefer to create an audio recording or even a vodcast. Regardless, students will need to practice reading their poems, which supports word recognition and reading fluency. Further, create a class book of poems based on the Poetry Café that includes illustrations or photographs, or share audio recordings or vodcasts on your class or school website.

Activities to Target Language

Poetry provides wonderful opportunities to teach language as well as to explore grammar, because poems often contain interesting sentence constructions that are less common in other genres. To achieve the language standards, we can provide mini-lessons on vocabulary or grammar specific to the poem we are reading. Poems are filled with wonderful and interesting words! After enjoying a poem, talk about the different words that the poet used and categorize them. For example, sort words into groups of nouns and verbs or adjectives and adverbs. Next, discuss and create a list of other words that the poet might have used. For example, rather than using *walk* a poet might use *stroll*, *saunter*, or *meander*. Asking students to walk in these different ways will help them to better understand the subtle differences in meaning and help them think about word choices. Likewise, students might rank order words (e.g., *teeny-weeny, tiny, small, big, bulky, colossal*). Although there probably will not be one correct order, the discussion that ensues will help students build deeper understandings of words. Afterward, rewrite several lines in the poem using different words and ask students to consider how the new poem makes them feel.

Poets also make up words, which can lead to interesting discussions. For example, Florian (2001) uses the made-up words "frogsicle" and "logsicle" in his poem "The Wood Frog" about a hibernating frog. After reading this poem aloud, ask students what they think these words mean and how the poet might have created those words. In addition to containing these and other made-up words, this poem includes the word *antifreeze*. After defining this word, you might lead students in a discussion about how animals can hibernate in cold weather but then wake up from their frozen slumber just fine.

SUMMARY

In this chapter, we considered the benefits and challenges of poetry read alouds and described ways to plan for a read aloud in order to minimize the challenges and maximize learning. We considered a different sequence for planning compared with that for literature and informational texts, because poetry can be intimidating at times. Finally, we described various anchor charts and activities to structure our read alouds of poetry to help students achieve various Common Core Standards.

ADDITIONAL POETRY RESOURCES

Collections

Hoberman, M. A., & Emberley, M. (2012). *Forget-me-nots: Poems to learn by heart.* New York, NY: Little, Brown Books for Young Readers.

Prelutsky, J., & Brown, M. (1986). *Read-aloud rhymes for the very young.* New York, NY: Knopf Books for Young Readers.

Favorite Children's Poets

Florian, D. (2002). *Insectlopedia.* Boston, MA: Houghton Mifflin.

Hoberman, M. A., & Emberley, M. (2006). *You read to me, I'll read to you: Very short stories to read together.* New York, NY: Little, Brown Books for Young Readers.

Hoberman, M. A., & Emberley, M. (2009). *You read to me, I'll read to you: Very short scary tales to read together.* New York, NY: Little, Brown Books for Young Readers.

Hoberman, M. A., & Emberley, M. (2010). *You read to me, I'll read to you: Very short fables to read together.* New York, NY: Little, Brown Books for Young Readers.

Additional Poetry Resources (continued)

Favorite Children's Poets (continued)

Hoberman, M. A., & Emberley, M. (2012). *You read to me, I'll read to you: Very short Mother Goose tales to read together.* New York, NY: Little, Brown Books for Young Readers.

Hoberman, M. A., & Emberley, M. (2014). *You read to me, I'll read to you: Very short tall tales to read together.* New York, NY: Little, Brown Books for Young Readers.

Prelutsky, J., & Stevenson, J. (2004). *It's raining pigs and noodles.* New York, NY: Greenwillow Books.

Prelutsky, J., Saint-Saens, C., & GrandPré, M. (2010). *The carnival of the animals.* New York, NY: Knopf Books for Young Readers.

Silverstein, S. (2006). *Falling up.* New York, NY: HarperCollins.

Silverstein, S. (2014). *A giraffe and a half.* New York, NY: HarperCollins.

Silverstein, S. (2015). *Runny babbit: A billy sook.* New York, NY: HarperCollins.

Multicultural

Alarcón, F. X., & Gonzalez, M. C. (2005). *From the bellybutton of the moon and other summer poems.* New York, NY: Children's Book Press.

Bruchac, J. (1997). *Thirteen moons on Turtle's back.* New York, NY: Puffin Books.

Greenfield, E., & Gilchrist, J. S. (2002) *Honey I love, and other love poems.* New York, NY: HarperCollins.

Kroll, V., & Roundtree, K. (1995). *Jaha and Jamil went down the hill: An African Mother Goose.* Watertown, MA: Charlesbridge.

Wright, D., & Acraman, H. (2012). *Japanese nursery rhymes: Carp streamer, falling rain, and other traditional favorites.* North Clarendon, VT: Tuttle.

Wright, D., & Acraman, H. (2013). *Korean nursery rhymes: Wild geese, land of goblins, and other favorite songs and rhymes.* North Clarendon, VT: Tuttle.

Wu, F., & Kieren Dutcher, K. (2010). *Chinese and English nursery rhymes: Share and sing in two languages.* North Clarendon, VT: Tuttle.

Internet Resources

www.gigglepoetry.com/
www.poetry4kids.com/
www.poetryfoundation.org/children/
www.poetryteachers.com/

CHAPTER 8

Digital Technologies

What do we mean by *digital technologies* and why would we include them in a book about reading aloud to students? First, digital technologies are electronic tools, devices, or systems that generate, store, or process information. Digital technologies include devices such as computers, laptops, tablets, e-readers, and cell phones. These technologies also include digital texts, which are electronic versions of a written text. For this chapter, we focus on electronic books, or e-books, that can be viewed on a computer or tablet (e.g., iPad).

E-books have many features similar to those of traditional books, such as print and pictures, and they tell a story or present information. However, they also have unique features, such as read-to-me, text highlighting, animation, sound effects, and hotspots. A hotspot is a specific object in an image that can be activated through touching or clicking on it. Most hotspots are animations and may include sound effects or music. E-books have the potential to support literacy and language development, but there are other reasons to consider digital technologies:

- Many students have access to digital technologies at home. They observe adults at home using technology to read and write, and it is natural for them to expect technology in schools.
- Digital technologies can increase students' engagement or persistence, and this supports learning (Moody, Justice, & Cabell, 2010).
- Reading digital text aloud helps students build a schema for interacting with multimodal texts and learning through technology (Labbo & Norguerón-Liu, 2014).
- Features such as text-to-speech or the read-to-me mode allow teachers to provide students with technology-supported practice.

Finally, the Common Core State Standards expect students to use technology to enhance their literacy, to support learning, and to understand the strengths and limitations of technological tools.

BENEFITS AND CHALLENGES OF USING E-BOOKS

As with traditional print books, reading e-books aloud introduces students to exciting adventures and new ideas. In addition, e-books open up other potential learning experiences. For example, videos embedded in informational e-books help students to observe the natural world in unique ways: Videos show animals in their natural habitats, and time-lapse videos show the growth of a plant or the metamorphosis of a caterpillar into a butterfly. E-books can be used to teach students basic technology skills such as clicking or swiping to turn pages or adjusting sound volume. They also can encourage students to gain more advanced technology skills such as the use of online references (e.g., a dictionary) and annotation tools (e.g., underlining or note-taking) that will benefit them in later grades.

During read alouds, using the read-to-me feature allows us to model this feature for students. Then, while the computer reads the text, we can observe more closely students' engagement and understanding. When this feature also highlights words, it supports developing print concept knowledge and reading skills and provides a model of fluent reading. After the read aloud, students can be encouraged to use the read-to-me feature to listen to the text again, which can be particularly helpful for students with learning differences. E-books offer additional supports for students with learning differences, such as the ability to change the font size for students with low vision, using earphones for students who are easily distracted, and accessing dictionary features for students with limited vocabulary or those learning English. Also, because some e-books can be read in a language other than English, this feature supports further development of students' home language and fosters biliteracy. Finally, e-books

- Reinforce early literacy skills (Korat, Shamir, & Arbiv, 2011)
- Foster talk about vocabulary (de Jong & Bus, 2002) and talk at high levels of cognitive thinking (Kim & Anderson, 2008)
- Aid text comprehension (Larson, 2010)
- Promote enthusiasm and persistence (Moody et al., 2010)
- Create moods and illustrate concepts through use of music and animation (Hoffman & Paciga, 2014)

There are also challenges when using e-books during read alouds. Locating high-quality e-books and avoiding gamelike texts is one challenge. Another challenge is finding time to learn how to operate features in an e-book in order to maximize learning and minimize distractions or technology glitches. Further, using e-books during read alouds requires that we alter our reading style to accommodate the affordances and limitations of digital texts, even if we use the read-to-me feature. During a read aloud, we want to teach students to use the electronic features, but we don't want that instruction to overshadow the content. We want to focus the talk on the content in the e-book. We also want to increase students' control of interactive digital features and decrease teacher control. To this end, students can take turns helping with e-book operation. Finally, we want to use e-books to supplement reading instruction, not to supplant reading instruction or reading practice. If students come to rely on technology to read for them, that decreases their opportunities to decode or identify meanings of words, and it reduces their willingness to take risks (Lefever-Davis & Pearman, 2005). As teachers, we have to create a balance in the classroom to capitalize on the benefits of e-books while minimizing the limitations.

As with literature, informational texts, and poetry, one way to achieve this balance is through intentional planning. Reflecting what we have set out in the previous chapters, we recommend the following five steps for planning:

1. Choose an e-book
2. Identify the learning objective(s)
3. Plan a method for introducing the e-book
4. Write questions and comments
5. Select anchor charts and activities

We suggest choosing an e-book before identifying the learning objective, because, initially, it may be challenging to find e-books of high quality. Of course, many, if not most, commercially produced curricula do include digital texts as well as online materials and resources. Those provide a good starting point.

CHOOSE AN E-BOOK

E-books and traditional print texts have much in common. However, e-books contain digital features that can support—or hinder—learning and enjoyment. Some e-books provide a high-quality educational experience that is so engaging and motivating for students that they don't even realize they are learning. Others contain poorly written text, present illustrations that are weak or even confusing, and have so many distracting features that they annoy most adults and make many teachers vow never to use them. This is unfortunate, but it speaks to the importance of choosing e-books with careful consideration.

Luckily, there is plenty of advice available to help us select quality e-books to use in the classroom. Based on the research, we compiled a summary of what to consider when choosing e-books and their various design features (see Figure 8.1; Morgan, 2013; Schugar, Smith, & Schugar, 2013; Shamir & Korat, 2009; Yokota & Teale, 2014). The key is to choose e-books that combine quality children's literature with the best of what digital features have to offer.

Figure 8.1. Questions to Answer When Selecting E-books to Use in the Classroom

Features to Consider	Questions to Answer
Navigation and Settings	Is it easy to see available features and set options?
	Is it easy to locate the forward, back, and pause buttons to move between screens?
	Does the e-book provide simple verbal directions to support the operation of the e-book and how to use features?
Digital Features	Is the font size large enough, or can it be resized?
	Do illustrations fit the screen's proportions?
	Are there read-to-me and print-highlighting features that support developing decoding skills? Are they easy to operate?
	In read-to-me mode, is the reader's voice pleasant? Does it convey an appropriate tone or represent characters accurately?
	Do the audio, images, animation, or interactive features/hotspots support or extend a reader's understanding of the text, or do they distract and confuse?
	Can the text be read in other languages to support students who are learning English?
Content	Is the story structure appropriate for students' abilities?
	Is the text well written with respect to the genre?
	Is the text skillfully crafted? Is the vocabulary interesting?
	Do the illustrations clearly support or extend the meaning of the text as a whole?
Educational Interactive Features	Can young students control their own interaction with the text?
	Do interactive features support a reader's ability to make inferences and understand vocabulary?
	Is there an interactive dictionary that provides child-friendly definitions?
	Are the interactive features strategically placed to enhance motivation, or do they detract from the text because they are too frequent or too time-consuming?
Entertainment Interactive Features	Are there entertainment features such as games, drawing/painting, videos, quizzes, or puzzles? If so, do they support or distract from the meaning of the text?
	Are entertainment features embedded in the text, or are they separate from the e-book?

Initially, find a few high-quality e-books that you enjoy and can envision using in the classroom. You just need to start somewhere! Where can one locate high-quality e-books in this age of digital overload? There are many helpful resources where you are likely to find the higher-quality options without having to sift through too many lower-quality varieties. Here are six places to start looking (listed in alphabetical order):

1. Digital Storytime (digital-storytime.com)
   - Collection of e-books and apps, some free and some at a small cost
   - Search by age of child, quality, languages available, price
   - Provides a screenshot and information about the book/app, including a review, star rating, synopsis, recommended age, video preview, and features available
2. The International Children's Digital Library (ICDL) (www.icdlbooks.org)
   - Online collection of books in nine languages
   - Search e-books by age range, genre, length, awards, language
3. PBS Kids Stories: Between the Lions (pbskids.org/lions/stories/)
   - Free online books; choose e-books based on genre
   - Read-to-me feature; highlights words; includes animations
4. Screen Actors Guild (SAG) Storyline (www.storylineonline.net)
   - Free online videos of actors reading a variety of stories
   - E-books presented in alphabetical order
5. StarWalk KidsMedia (starwalkkids.com/)
   - Collection of high-quality fiction and nonfiction trade books at a cost for families or schools
   - Search by title, author, key word, grade, or reading level
   - The Teaching Links feature matches each e-book to relevant Common Core State Standards and suggests activities
6. TumbleBooks Library (www.tumblebooks.com)
   - Collection of animated, talking picture books; cost for families or schools but often accessible through local library
   - Search by title, author, reading level, or new additions
   - Provides information on Common Core State Standards; includes quizzes, games, videos, book report forms, and lesson plans

Finally, talk with your media specialist to learn what other resources your district may have already purchased.

IDENTIFY THE LEARNING OBJECTIVE(S)

The next step in planning a read aloud is to identify a learning objective, or more than one. A learning objective might be a Common Core State Standard or may come from the district curriculum. We also suggest you consider the standards from the International Society for Technology in Education (ISTE; www.iste.org). Broadly, these student standards address (a) creativity and innovation; (b) communication and collaboration; (c) research and information fluency; (d) critical thinking, problem solving, and decisionmaking; (e) digital citizenship; and (f) technology and operations concepts. The ISTE standards were created to help ensure that students gain the technology skills necessary for functioning in the current and future technological environment.

PLAN A METHOD FOR INTRODUCING THE E-BOOK

Echoing what we do with other genres, when introducing an e-book, we need to consider (a) the learning objective, (b) the needs of the students in the class, and (c) the features of the e-book. However, because e-books have unique digital features, there are other issues to consider before, during, and after an e-book read aloud.

Before reading an e-book, we have some logistical decisions to make about how to project it and what interactive features to model. Will the students view the e-book from a device, see it projected onto a screen, or see it, if possible, on an interactive whiteboard? If the e-book is to be projected, prior to reading aloud, ensure compatibility between the device and the projection method and make sure the technology works. Make sure students can hear the reader if you use the read-to-me feature. Also consider the logistics of interactive (e.g., clicking or swiping to turn the page, hotspots) and digital features (e.g., sound, narration). If the e-book has a read-to-me feature, consider using it so that you can observe students' reactions to the text. Also, consider whether to enable or disable features such as sound, animation, or text highlighting. Plan whether to activate all, some, or none of the hotspots during the read aloud. What kind of discussion might ensue after a hotspot is activated? Will that add to or distract from the flow of the text? It is helpful to model and discuss such interactive features when reading e-books so that students can learn how to use them effectively. While some students will be familiar with e-books, all students can benefit from instruction on how these features can support or distract them. Some students might benefit from small-group instruction to guide their ability to use such technological tools.

Finally, introducing the e-book is not unlike introducing other types of texts (for ideas, see the chapters on literature, informational texts, and poetry). If the text is story or informational text, describe the purpose of this read aloud. If the text is a poem, help students focus on the aesthetics first, and then on a second or third reading, move on to an academic purpose for reading it. If you plan to use a picture walk with students, decide whether to conduct the picture walk with the sound or animation on or off. A picture walk without the sound or animation helps students focus on the content rather than the technology. Alternatively, a picture walk with the sound and animation on could stimulate a different discussion about the content. Try each option as you begin to use e-books in the classroom and decide how each approach serves your purposes.

WRITE QUESTIONS AND COMMENTS

The next step is to plan several questions to ask or comments to make during the read aloud. Determine questions that will help students achieve the learning objectives and the purpose for each read aloud. E-books do not necessitate a different approach; instead, consider the genre of text. See the chapters on literature, informational text, and poetry to help write questions, and refer to Figure 3.3 to identify ways to Raise the Bar depending on the genre of the text. Obviously, posting sticky notes on the appropriate pages is not an option in an e-book. The e-book may have an electronic version of a sticky note, or you will need to jot down questions on paper.

SELECT ANCHOR CHARTS AND ACTIVITIES

Choose anchor charts and activities based on the genre of the text and the learning objectives. Many of the anchor charts and activities presented in Chapters 5, 6, and 7 will be useful with e-books. However, e-books also provide different opportunities for multimedia and multimodal activities. Multimedia activities involve the use of different types of media such as text, still images, videos, audio, or interactive content. Multimodal activities involve oral and written language (linguistics), still and moving images (visual), music and sound effects (audio), body language and facial expressions (gestural), and objects in space (spatial). We suggest the following three methods for integrating multimedia and multimodal activities into e-book read alouds.

Digital Language Experience Approach

In a Digital Language Experience Approach (D-LEA), teachers and students use a computer or tablet along with images or recordings to author printed books or e-books (which can include audio narration) about their own experiences. The approach is based on the Language Experience Approach, but uses a variety of digital resources. See the online article by Labbo, Eakle, and Montero (2002), which describes the four steps of this approach with great examples. Briefly, here are the four steps.

Set up the experience. The teacher and students identify an experience to write about and create a plan for taking photographs. For example, if the class is going on a field trip to a local pizza restaurant, decide what types of photos will be needed in order to create the e-book on your return. Also decide who will take photos on the field trip and who will direct the photographing. If the e-book will include video, make a plan for what videos might be interesting.

It is helpful to think in advance about what photos and videos would create a good story, but we also have to be alert during the experience and notice opportunities that present themselves.

Photograph the experience. As students engage in the experience, the teacher, students, or both take photographs with a digital camera. Multiple cameras can be helpful to get different perspectives. If photos of each student are needed, one student can be in charge of a checklist to mark off which photos are completed. For the pizza shop example, the teacher may be the designated photographer and take photos that represent the sequence of events (e.g., photos of the tour of the restaurant, small groups of students making their own personal pizzas, everyone eating lunch). Perhaps include a short video of the chef throwing the pizza crust high in the air.

Compose the multimedia story or photo essay. After images and video are downloaded onto a computer or tablet, the class reviews and discusses them and their experience. With support, students select the images they believe best represent the experience and arrange them in a sequence. Students can dictate their thoughts for their teacher to type, or type text themselves. Revisions are made after the teacher reads the text aloud. Next, the teacher, students, or both read the text aloud and record the narration. Students listen to the recording to determine if changes are needed to the text or recording. Finally, depending on the software, students might add multimedia features such as music or sound effects.

Share and enjoy the story. Once complete, the story is published. Most software has options for creating e-books and printing the book. Therefore, students and teachers can interact with the book in various ways. The teacher can read the digital text aloud or use the audio narration. Students can be encouraged to read the text through choral or echo reading. With the audio narration, students can independently listen or read along. Printed copies of the book can be available in the classroom library or checked out to share at home, or e-books can be shared with families.

Apps to consider using within the D-LEA approach include Storybuddy, by Tapfuze; and Story Creator, by Innovative Mobile Apps.

Digital Storytelling

Digital storytelling is another exciting way to engage students in multimedia projects. While the D-LEA approach focuses on experiences, digital storytelling can be used to encourage story creation. The process is not unlike that described for D-LEA. Bogard and McMackin (2012) provide the following suggestions for helping students engage in digital storytelling.

Plan and develop a story. An important step in the writing process is brainstorming ideas, and this is no different when using technology. Students can be encouraged to complete a graphic organizer or draw simple pictures to stimulate ideas. Next, students can create an outline of their ideas using text or drawings, or both, and then begin to write a draft of their stories. However, by using technology, students can also record their ideas for their stories. Then they can listen to their stories and modify or elaborate ideas as they write it down. Finally, students decide what materials they need to collect, such as drawings, photos, videos, audio recordings, and music.

Listen, think critically, and confer. An important part of the writing process is revising, including receiving feedback from a peer or teacher. Before producing their story in digital form, students confer with peers to get feedback on their ideas. Students can share their story ideas with a peer, and also share their drawings, sequence, and any audio notes they have created. By answering their peers' questions and listening to their suggestions, students can make revisions to their story ideas.

Create and produce the story. After receiving feedback from peers on their ideas, students create or finalize the storyboard they will use in producing the digital story. Students prepare their media (e.g., scanned drawings, images, videos) and start adding them to their digital story. A variety of software is available for producing digital stories. A common video editing software is iMovie, which comes on all Mac computers; PhotoStory is readily available for Windows-based computers. The apps mentioned above for the D-LEA are options. In addition, StoryBird (storybird.com/) and Little Bird Tales (littlebirdtales.com/) are both options for digital storytelling. Once students have learned to use the software, they can arrange their images or video clips and add narration and, if desired, music. Now students are ready to share their digital stories.

Digital Research Project

A good multimedia option for curricular topics and informational texts is producing a digital research project. Students choose a topic and a purpose for their project (e.g., to inform or persuade). They consider their audience and what that audience needs to know. They can generate questions that help them focus their project. For example, if a current science theme is plants, a group of students could focus on the question "What do plants need in order to grow?" They would search for information on what plants need in order to stay healthy.

Students will need help learning to locate resources appropriate for their abilities as they research a topic. Print resources can be available in the classroom on the curricular topic. Some online resources for students include BrainPOP Jr. (jr.brainpop.com), Kids.gov (kids.usa.gov/), GoPebble (www.pebblego.com), and National Geographic Kids (kids.nationalgeographic.com/videos/). Students also need instruction and support on how to collect information from various sources. Teachers can provide graphic organizers or note-taking frames for students to use as they gather information. As needed, teach mini-lessons about using text structure and text features to locate information, identifying main ideas and important details, distinguishing between facts and opinions, organizing information, and summarizing.

Once students have completed their research, they write text, draw pictures, or locate images and videos to create the sequence of information they plan to include in their final product. They can do this on paper first, or use the software/app they will use to publish their research project. As with any writing project, students will need to receive feedback and make revisions. Software/apps that might be used to present a research project include Glogster (glogster.edu), which is a virtual poster, or Book Creator (redjumper.net).

As a culminating event, be sure to create a forum for sharing their final research projects with the class and then outside the class (e.g., with another class, with school administrators, with families). Send out invitations to the event. Help students prepare how they will introduce their projects prior to sharing them. Give audience members an opportunity to ask questions after each presentation. Create a celebratory atmosphere as you showcase students' accomplishments.

SUMMARY

In this chapter, we considered the benefits and challenges of using digital texts and described ways to plan for a read aloud in order to minimize the challenges and maximize learning. Sharing e-books as part of read alouds is a first step in using digital tools in the classroom. Therefore, we described activities that provide additional opportunities for students to create their own multimedia and multimodal texts. This is not simply using technology because it is popular or engaging for students; such activities support students in achieving the Common Core State Standards of producing and publishing their own writing, collaborating with peers, and learning to use multimedia and digital tools.

CHAPTER 9

Accommodating Students with Learning Differences

Reading aloud benefits *all* students regardless of learning differences. In fact, many of the read aloud strategies discussed in this book help to ensure that students with learning differences will be successful during read alouds. Nevertheless, there are additional ways to ensure that students with learning differences will learn from whole-class and small-group read alouds. In this chapter, we discuss methods for supporting students who are ELLs as well as students with other learning differences, such as speech and language impairments, learning disabilities, intellectual disabilities, autism, and complex communication needs (i.e., those who use augmentative and alternative communication devices). Specifically, we explore three types of accommodations that can support students with learning differences during read alouds: (a) structural accommodations, (b) textual accommodations, and (c) interactional accommodations.

STRUCTURAL ACCOMMODATIONS

Students with learning differences may benefit from structures different from those we currently use in our classroom. We can consider altering the physical structures and the routines we use for read alouds to better support students' individual needs. When planning for students with learning differences, consider which of these structural accommodations will maximize success for the particular students in the class.

Seating Arrangements

Students with learning differences will vary in their needs for a seating arrangement during read alouds. Although our typical seating arrangement may be on the floor, this may create challenges for some students. Students who are prone to distraction or who have difficulty with behavioral regulation may be more successful if they are seated in chairs at their desks or at a table during a read aloud. Such seating makes it clear where their bodies should be. Desks or chairs also limit physical interaction with other students, which can reduce distractions.

Alternatively, some students with sensory issues may need more sensory stimulation in order to attend and participate. For example, for some, sitting in a rocking chair or beanbag chair, or holding a manipulative (sometimes called a fidget object) during the read aloud can increase their ability to attend and verbally participate. Experimenting with various options can help determine which is most effective for particular students. Consult other professionals in the school who support students with learning differences, such as an occupational therapist, physical therapist, special education teacher, speech-language pathologist, vision specialist, guidance counselor, and a teacher of English to speakers of other languages (TESOL).

Group Size

Group size is another consideration for those with learning differences. Read alouds often include the entire class; however, students with learning differences can benefit from read alouds in smaller groups. With fewer students in the group, the teacher can tailor book choices, alter the text while reading, and scaffold better student responses during the discussion. Furthermore, students will have more opportunities to talk, and that can improve attention and comprehension.

Yet smaller group sizes can be hard to achieve. Some teachers choose to read first to the whole class, but then later read the same text a second time in small groups with students with learning differences. A specialist or paraprofessional can be recruited to read to a small group of students, too. However, be sure students with learning differences are read to by a person who can best support their needs. Small groups may vary in size; for example, the teacher could read to 15 students while the TESOL teacher reads to the 7 students who are ELLs or have other learning differences.

Visual Supports

Visual supports are useful for all students; however, for students with learning differences, visual supports can make all the difference (e.g., Britsch, 2010; Facella, Rampino, & Shea, 2005). Visuals can include the photographs or illustrations in a book, objects/props, anchor charts, or gestural cues. Consider the anchor charts described in Chapters 5, 6, and 7 that can support students with learning differences. However, visual supports may or may not make sense to students automatically. Therefore, it is important to explain how to use them rather than leave students to infer how to use them (see Lanter & Watson, 2008). For example, in order for a Venn diagram to be helpful, we need to explain to students where we write similarities and where we write the differences. We also need to model how to use the contents of the Venn diagram to help students talk about the topic.

Repeated Exposure to the Text

Repeated reading of a text is beneficial for all students, but it is particularly important for students with learning differences (e.g., Restrepo, Morgan, & Thompson, 2013). It provides multiple exposures to new vocabulary, grammar, and content, and gives teachers additional opportunities to scaffold students' understanding. Many of the texts read aloud to students in preschool through 2nd grade reasonably can be read multiple times. Alternatively, routines for repeated readings could be achieved through the following options.

Access to e-books. Using audiobooks or e-books in the classroom (see Shamir, Korat, & Fellah, 2012) or at home (see below; Koskinen et al., 2000) can be an excellent way to make repeated readings possible. Be sure students know how to activate the read-to-me feature and text highlighting. Avoid e-books with many game components (see Chapter 8 for considerations for choosing e-books).

Small-group readings with a teacher, specialist, volunteer, or peer buddy. Planning for exposure to the text, either prior to or after a whole-class read aloud, can help students with learning differences. Such repeated readings could be led by a teacher, adult volunteer, or peer buddy. If the small-group reading is led by an adult, it can result in more opportunities for students with learning differences to talk and the adult scaffolding needed to help them talk in more sophisticated ways (Koskinen et al., 2000). The focus during such small groups can be on teaching target vocabulary, reinforcing important concepts for comprehension, and encouraging retelling. If peer buddies or volunteers lead the read aloud, students at least become familiar with the language and content in the text. For ELLs, it can be beneficial to provide opportunities to read with a speaker of the students' home language (Gillanders & Castro, 2011).

Home read alouds. As mentioned above, repeated readings can be achieved through a home reading component. We can send the text home with students to be read by a parent, caregiver, or sibling. A text in the student's home language is a great option when that is available. Alternatively, we can send home audio recordings or e-books, especially if the student will complete the task independently. A home reading component could also include teaching parents to use a responsive style of interaction. Parents can learn simple strategies to use during book reading at home to facilitate verbal participation, either in English or in their home language for those who are ELLs (Binger,

Kent-Walsh, Berens, Del Campo, & Rivera, 2008). Teachers can use the ideas in Table 2.1 to contrast a responsive versus a directive style and help parents practice while reading with their own child.

Alternative Follow-Up Activities

After reading a text aloud in the classroom, teachers often engage students in additional reading, writing, and hands-on activities related to the text. Although students with learning differences may benefit from these follow-up activities, they may need modifications or different activities altogether. For example, after reading a few information books on frogs, students in the classroom may be drawing and labeling their own diagrams of a frog's life cycle. Students with learning differences, however, may benefit much more by working with their teacher, a paraprofessional, or a speech-language pathologist in a small-group session that is tailored to their needs. Instead of generating their own diagrams, students might learn much more from putting pictures into a life cycle sequence and then explaining the sequence of changes with adult scaffolding for content and language. Alternatively, students might benefit from the reteaching of target vocabulary and a frog's life cycle word sort activity that includes those words to build deeper word knowledge.

Structural accommodations can include making changes to seating or group size, adding visual supports or opportunities for repeated readings, or planning for alternative follow-up activities. Picking even just one or two of these structural changes to read alouds can help students with learning differences be more successful.

TEXTUAL ACCOMMODATIONS

Students with learning differences benefit greatly from being included in classrooms with their same-age peers who are typically developing. While these students are often included in whole-class read alouds of books that do not match their level of ability, there is value in including them in those sessions. However, teachers also can assist students with learning differences, especially those with significant disabilities, by (a) choosing alternative texts or (b) adapting the text itself.

Choose Alternative Texts

First, students with learning differences may need different texts from those used with the rest of the class. Teachers could choose different books on the same curricular topic but with language and content that more closely match the students' abilities (Lanter & Watson, 2008). For students with the most significant disabilities, consider the benefits of the following types of books:

- Books with repeated lines or rhyming patterns can help facilitate participation (Browder, Mims, Spooner, Ahlgrim-Delzell, & Lee, 2008).
- Patterned books provide scaffolds that are built into the text, such as alphabet books, counting books, add-on stories, and good-bad/good-bad patterns. Such patterns provide cues for the listener and support memory and comprehension. See Zipprich, Grace, and Grote-Garcia (2009) for descriptions of various types of patterned books.
- Books with flaps help facilitate engagement and visual attention because the student can manipulate the pages (Kaderavek & Justice, 2005; Vogler-Elias, 2009).

Such alternative texts selected for students with learning differences could be read aloud prior to a whole-class read aloud, providing pre-exposure to the same topic. Content that overlaps in both texts could be highlighted during the whole-class read aloud, and students with learning differences could then participate verbally or through whatever means they use to communicate (e.g., picture boards, computer voice output devices).

Another option for alternative texts is to select books that match the student's specific interests. For example, books on shells and ocean creatures might be a good choice for a 2nd-grade student with autism who is fascinated with this topic. Specialists such as speech-language pathologists and special education teachers can assist in selecting or providing books that match the students' abilities and interests. Such alternative texts could be useful for small-group teacher-led read alouds and for reading with a peer. Although these texts will not necessarily match the curricular topic, they can meet the students' educational goals more successfully than the texts used with the whole class.

Adapt the Text

Another option teachers have is to use the same book chosen for the class, but to adapt the text. If the text is too long, we can shorten it by reading it in smaller segments at a time, or omitting some segments altogether. We just need to be careful that the text remains comprehensible without the omitted text. We also could reduce the cognitive demands of a text by simplifying the language, using more familiar synonyms, or adding explanations when inferences are required (Dodd, 2012). For example, in the book *Who Eats What? Food Chains and Food Webs* (Lauber & Keller, 1995), the text tells how a caterpillar eats a leaf, a wren eats the caterpillar, and a hawk eats the wren. Students are expected to infer the food chain hierarchy, so we could add an explicit explanation of that sequence. We also could adapt the text to provide more exposures to a target word or concept. For example, we could preteach the concept of a food chain and then, during the read aloud, add more uses of that term into the reading. Such additions could triple the number of exposures to that concept. It is important to identify how to adapt a text prior to the read aloud. Difficult concepts and inferences are best identified ahead of time. Sticky notes can be helpful as a reminder of the plan to alter the text or where to add explanations or vocabulary.

INTERACTIONAL ACCOMMODATIONS

Our focus in this book is on achieving a responsive-interactive read aloud. For students with learning differences, entering into the dialogue can be challenging; and yet dialogue provides an important learning tool (Lanter & Watson, 2008; Restrepo et al., 2013). Responsiveness is a key ingredient for helping students with learning differences participate successfully during a read aloud.

The reality is, however, that adults have a hard time providing scaffolding with students with language and learning differences (McGinty, Justice, Zucker, Gosse, & Skibbe, 2012). Our tendency is to become more directive and less responsive with students with learning differences compared with students who are typically developing. Such a tendency is understandable because students' contributions may be difficult to interpret. Therefore, teachers often ask multiple closed-ended questions in an attempt to decipher students' meaning. Unfortunately, using a directive approach drives students with learning differences to become passive and less interactive. In fact, some students become minimally responsive to all these questions. How can we avoid contributing to these students' difficulties? What interactional strategies can we apply? Four recommendations can improve the success of our students with learning differences:

- Maximize a positive climate through responsiveness
- Plan prompts for students to enter the discussion
- Clarify with Low-Support Strategies
- Follow up with High-Support Strategies

Maximize a Positive Climate Through Responsiveness

Students with learning differences can be hesitant to verbally participate or take risks in a classroom. A responsive style creates a climate that is positive and that encourages these students to participate verbally. Although typically developing students participate even when the adult is not highly responsive in style, students with learning differences participate at above-average levels only when the adult is highly supportive and responsive (Rabidoux & MacDonald, 2000; Skibbe, Moody, Justice, & McGinty, 2010). Therefore, the best way to achieve the kind of positive climate these students need is to achieve a high degree of responsiveness.

What would that look like? The strategies listed in Figure 2.1 are useful. Use comments, follow the student's topic, allow wait time, keep a slow pace, and strive for balance in the number of teacher and student turns. When questions are needed, be sure they are genuine, topic-continuing, and open-ended. These strategies help create a climate in which students with learning differences feel comfortable participating.

Plan Prompts for Students to Enter the Discussion

Students with learning differences often need help entering the discussion during a read aloud. Students with the most significant needs are put at a disadvantage when they cannot secure turns on their own (Trudeau, Cleave, & Woelk, 2003). During our planning for a read aloud, there are three ways we can assist students to enter the discussion:

Raise the Bar questions. We suggest that teachers plan several Raise the Bar questions prior to a read aloud that can initiate a discussion. Remember that many students with learning differences are capable of handling high levels of cognitive thinking, even when they struggle with the language to express those ideas. Raise the Bar questions get students talking, and then teachers can follow up with Low-Support and High-Support Strategies to scaffold better responses.

Open-ended prompts. Teachers can plan open-ended prompts to help students enter the discussion. Here are some examples of open-ended prompts:

- "Tell me what happened on this page."
- "Tell me about one of the characters in this story."
- "Tell me something about how a tadpole changes into a frog."
- "Tell me how this poem made you feel."

The open-ended nature of the prompts makes students more willing to participate. They are more likely to be successful, because many responses would be considered correct.

High-Support Strategies. Finally, with students who have the most significant learning differences, High-Support Strategies can be helpful right from the start. For example, a teacher might choose to start by eliciting imitations; asking students to point, gesture, or pantomime; or asking fill-in-the-blank, yes/no, or forced-choice questions. These strategies limit the amount of language required and, therefore, students achieve quick success.

Clarify with Low-Support Strategies

When our students with learning differences make ambiguous comments during a read aloud, it can be difficult to know what type of support to choose. In this situation, immediately providing High Support can be detrimental because we might miss the student's point entirely. That would invalidate the student's contribution, redirecting it to our own agenda. Thus, we fail to follow the student's lead and build on his or her original idea. Our directive rather than responsive approach may serve to shut the student down in the moment, or worse, it may reduce the student's willingness to participate in the future. The student ends up misunderstood and unsuccessful, which contributes to a cycle of failure over time.

Therefore, when a student's contribution is ambiguous, the best approach is to request clarification (see Low-Support Strategies in Figure 3.3). Low-Support Strategies that provide a second chance or that request clarification keep the student in charge of his or her idea. As the student elaborates, the teacher will have sufficient information to determine whether to proceed using High, Low, or Raise-the-Bar Support. For example, if the student's elaboration is correct and includes appropriate language, the teacher can respond using a Raise-the-Bar Strategy. Alternatively, if the student's elaboration contains content and language errors, the teacher can respond with High Support that is responsive in nature and builds on the student's original idea.

Follow Up with High-Support Strategies

High-Support Strategies are an important teaching tool for students with learning differences. Students with learning differences can gesture or point, imitate, fill in the blank, answer yes/no and forced-choice questions, and answer comprehension-check questions. Such High-Support Strategies ensure that students learn language and content and also prevent students from failing in front of their peers. Such support can contribute to positive peer perceptions of the student with learning differences.

In addition to the High-Support Strategies we suggest in Figure 3.2, students with learning differences can benefit from additional High-Support Strategies.

- Provide rich explanations for words. Model new words and define them by giving child-friendly definitions. Use synonyms, point to illustrations, and use the word in a new sentence. Rich explanation is especially helpful for students with learning differences in learning new words (Collins, 2010).
- Elicit imitations of new words. Asking students to imitate a new word helps them create a phonological imprint (Beck & McKeown, 2007).
- Model and encourage gestures. Modeling gestures helps students understand the language they hear, and encouraging them to use gestures while they talk aids in word learning and retention (Singleton & Saks, 2015). Teachers can include gestures that show the shape or function associated with a word. For example, when discussing the meaning of the word "leap," add a gesture (e.g., two fingers bouncing off palm of your hand) and encourage students to imitate the gesture.
- Provide specific feedback. Tell students what was accurate and what was inaccurate about their contribution. Include the following information:
  » Praise—validate the student's contribution (e.g., "Great you told me a characteristic of frogs—they have webbed feet")
  » Correction—fix what was incorrect (e.g., "They have webbed feet—not webbed foot—say webbed feet")
- Provide time to prepare an answer. Enforce wait time prior to asking students to give responses (Facella et al., 2005). For example, present a question to the whole class. Ask students to think of a response but not to say anything yet. Then call on a student with a learning difference.
- Provide time to practice. Ask students to share their answer to a question with a shoulder buddy. Then ask a student with a learning difference to share the answers they discussed.
- Protect the student's turn. Restrict other students from commenting or interrupting (e.g., "It's April's turn; we're listening for April's idea").
- Use attention-getters. Give prompts to look at or notice something in the book so that students with learning differences will stay focused and attending (Vogler-Elias, 2009).
- Encourage role-playing or acting out. Give students opportunities to act out or role-play. This expands the concept of gesturing and pointing and is particularly useful for students learning English or who have language impairment (Gillanders & Castro, 2011).

SUMMARY

In this chapter, we described three types of accommodations we can make to support students with learning differences, including structural accommodations, textual accommodations, and interactional accommodations. Applying these accommodations can support our students who are ELLs or who have disabilities so that they increase their willingness to participate during read alouds. As students participate more, teachers have more opportunities to scaffold better and better responses. By using responsive-interactive read aloud scaffolding strategies, along with these additional accommodations, we can assist students in co-creating meaning during the read aloud to reach higher levels of language and content knowledge than they could achieve independently.

Two Example Text Sets with Learning Objectives and Reading Session Guides

TEXT SET 1

Target Grade: Preschool or Kindergarten; Topic: Frogs

Tale of a Tadpole, by Karen Wallace (Informational Text)
A Frog Thing, by Eric Drachman, illustrated by James Muscarello (Literature)
Lizards, Frogs, and Polliwogs, by Douglas Florian, reading the poem "The Polliwogs"
(p. 30; Poetry)

Learning Objectives

- With prompting and support, ask and answer questions about key details in a text; story elements (literature); life cycle of frogs (informational text)
- Ask and answer questions about unknown words; indicate that verbs are action words and use target verbs from each text
- Make predictions and inferences while listening to a text
- With prompting and support, identify basic similarities and differences between stories, informational texts, and poems

First Session—*A Frog Thing* (Literature)

1. Introduce the text and the following purposes for this read aloud:
   a. To make predictions
   b. To recall and use target verbs from the story
2. During the read aloud, identify story elements and target verbs by acting out/gesturing/pantomiming: *jumped, leapt, dove* (in water), *flapped, flopped,*

swooped (in water), *coughed, wheezed, shrugged, glided, swooped* (in air), *dove* (in air)

3. During the read aloud, make predictions/inferences at predetermined places within the text:
   a. How do you think Frank felt when everyone was laughing at him? (inference) What do you see in the illustrations that support your idea? (use illustrations to support thinking)
   b. Do you think Frank will be able to learn to fly? Why or why not? (prediction)
   c. How do you think the mommy bird felt when her baby fell in the water? (inference)
   d. Do you think the mommy bird will help Frank fly? How? (prediction)
   e. How do you think Frank feels as he is flying through the air? (inference) What in the text or illustrations helps you know that? (use text/illustrations to support thinking)
4. After the read aloud, ask two Raise the Bar questions:
   a. At the end of the story, Frank decides that he will try to become a great swimmer and not try to fly anymore. Why? What did he learn from his experience with the birds? (point of view of a character)
   b. Is there something you would like to do but it isn't a "person thing"? Share with the class. (experiential connection)
5. After the read aloud, teach the target verbs: *jumped, leapt, dove* (in water), *flapped, flopped, swooped* (in water), *coughed, wheezed, shrugged, glided, swooped* (in air), *dove* (in air)
   a. Look at what Frank is doing in the illustrations
   b. Pantomime and act out each word and discuss word meanings

Second Session—*A Frog Thing* (Literature)

1. Introduce the text and the following purposes for this read aloud:
   a. To identify story elements
   b. To recall and use target verbs from the story
2. After reading aloud, map out story using story grammar anchor chart
   a. Characters (Frank, his parents, baby bird, mommy bird, his frog friends)
   b. Setting (pond, on the bank of the pond, in the sky)
   c. Goal/main problem (Frank wants to fly even though it is not a frog thing)
   d. Events (Frank tries everything he can to fly; saves the baby bird who falls into pond; mother bird is very grateful and wants to do something nice for Frank)
   e. Resolution (Frank gets to experience flying when the mommy bird

and another bird fly while he holds on to a stick; Frank's friends and parents are amazed that he really got to fly)

3. After the read aloud, act out/gesture/pantomime the target verbs: *jumped, leapt, dove* (in water), *flapped, flopped, swooped* (in water), *coughed, wheezed, shrugged, glided, swooped* (in air), *dove* (in air); fill in the vocabulary connections chart for several target verbs.

Third Session—*Tale of a Tadpole* (Informational Text)

1. Introduce the text and the following purposes for this read aloud:
   a. To notice illustrations and identify three informational text features
   b. To sequence the steps in the life cycle of a frog
   c. To learn target vocabulary
2. During the read aloud:
   a. Identify and explain the three informational text features as they appear (photo insets, picture word list, index).
   b. Explain the noun vocabulary as it appears in the text (*tadpole, froglet, gills, webbed toes, flippers*).
   c. Stop for each target verb to discuss the meaning of the word and act out/pantomime/gesture to show the meaning visually (*escape, nibble, gobble, shrink, creep, snatch*)
   d. Ask two Raise the Bar questions:
      i. Why do the tadpoles hide in the weeds?
      ii. How are we the same as or different from a tadpole? From a frog?
   e. Use line drawings or props to create a flow chart showing the sequence of steps in the life cycle of a frog as you read.
3. After the read aloud:
   a. Show a video that follows the eggs as they hatch into tadpoles and gradually change into frogs (www.youtube.com/watch?v=wAcwjWi6I9Y, 7-minute video titled "From Egg to Frog in 7 Weeks" that shows changes over 49 days; or www.youtube.com/watch?v=AMs3waaW75g, 3-minute video titled "Life Cycle of a Frog!" that combines video and cartoon animation).
   b. Students retell the life cycle sequence using the completed flow chart; assist students in using target vocabulary

Fourth Session—*Tale of a Tadpole* (Informational Text)

1. Introduce the text and the following purposes for this read aloud:
   a. To use illustrations and text features
   b. To sequence the steps in the life cycle of a frog

   c. To recall and use target vocabulary

   d. To identify basic similarities and differences between informational texts and storybooks

2. While reading, ask students to recall information from *Tale of a Tadpole*. To support recall, tell students that text features can help us learn and remember information. Review the book and identify features that help us learn and remember information.

3. After reading, use illustrations and text in the book to answer the question "How does an egg/tadpole turn into a frog?" Use the props to show each stage of the life cycle. Find information in the text to answer the question "What do frogs need to live and grow?" Draw and write students' responses on a large sheet of paper, marker board, or smart board. See the example concept map in Figure 6.4.

4. Identify basic similarities and differences between informational text and storybook. Walk through the pages of the informational text and then the story. Create a T-chart to compare story and informational text:

   • Story: not real, tell a story, include characters, animals might talk, illustrations are often artwork

   • Informational: real, give information or facts, often include photographs, picture word list/glossary

Fifth Session—*Lizards, Frogs, and Polliwogs*, Poem Titled "The Polliwogs" (p. 30)

1. Introduce the poem and the following aesthetic purposes for the first read aloud:

   a. To visualize and use our senses and imaginations while experiencing the poem

   b. To listen for the rhythms in the lines of poetry

2. Read the poem aloud—explain first that a tadpole is also called a polliwog.

   a. Do not show the illustration during the first reading. Ask students to close their eyes while they listen to the poem and to visualize and imagine in their minds what they see, hear, smell, taste, or feel.

   b. After reading the poem, ask students to share what they imagined. Consider all five senses. Act out the movements of the tadpoles.

3. Move from an aesthetic purpose to your academic purposes. Watch a segment of the time-lapse video again showing the tadpoles moving quickly in the water (minute 3:40 to 3:50). Have students describe to a shoulder buddy what they saw the tadpoles doing. Then explain the following purposes for the next reading:

   a. To notice the words the author used to describe the movements of the tadpoles

     b. To describe the font and placement of words and letters on the page and consider the author's reasons for choosing them

     c. To describe what the artwork adds to the words

4. After the reading, ask the following Raise the Bar questions:

     a. What words in the poem help you imagine the tadpoles moving? How are *quiver, shiver, jiggle,* and *jog* similar in meaning? How are they different? Let's put them in order.

     b. What did the author do to the letters on the page? Why do you suppose the author put the words on the page in this way? What does it make you think of when you look at the text?

     c. What does the artwork make you think when you look at it? What does it add to the poet's words?

TEXT SET 2

Target Grade: 2nd grade;
Topic: Overcoming hardship to pursue a dream

Amazing Grace, by Mary Hoffman and Caroline Binch (1991) (Literature)
A Chair for My Mother, by Vera B. Williams (1982) (Literature)

Learning Objectives:

- Recount stories to determine central message
- Describe and compare and contrast how characters in a story respond to major events and challenges
- Describe differences in the characters' points of view
- Use information gained from the illustrations and text to demonstrate understanding of its characters, setting, or plot
- Compare and contrast stories with a similar theme
- Identify hardships we have or might encounter and how we have or could respond

First Session—*Amazing Grace* (Literature)

1. Introduce the text and the following purposes for this read aloud:

     a. To learn target vocabulary

     b. To map out the story elements

2. During reading, stop to teach the target vocabulary. Select several words from the story:

     a. Nouns: *adventure, auditions, success, performance*

     b. Adjectives: *sparkling, stunning, stellar*

3. After reading, complete a story map anchor chart:
   a. Characters (Grace, her mom, her nana)
   b. Setting (home and school)
   c. Goal/main problem (Grace wants to be Peter Pan in her classroom's show; other kids say she cannot be Peter Pan because she is a girl or because she is Black)
   d. Events (Nana takes her to a show where the star is a Black woman; Grace practices hard; she wins the part)
   e. Resolution (Grace gives a stellar performance and changes the minds of her peers)

Second Session—*Amazing Grace* (Literature)

1. Introduce the text with the following purposes for this read aloud:
   a. To describe how different characters respond to the problem
   b. To recount the story to identify the central message
2. Recount the story *Amazing Grace* using the story map from session one and the book illustrations as visual supports
3. After recounting the story, ask Raise the Bar questions. These focus on the central message and how characters respond to problems, which are the learning objectives.
   a. How did Grace feel when the kids said those things? How did her mother feel? (inferences) What do you see in the illustrations that support your answer? (use illustrations to support thinking)
   b. How did her mother respond when Grace told her about what the kids at school had said? How did her nana respond? How were their responses similar or different? (compare/contrast within text)
   c. What did Nana want Grace to learn by going to the ballet? (inferences) What in the illustrations or text makes you think that? (use text/illustrations to support thinking)
   d. How did Grace change by the end of the story? (explain text features—character change over time given her goals and challenges)
   e. What does this story teach us? (central message, experiential connection) (we all face hardships; we have a choice in how we respond to hardships; if we work hard we can achieve what we want; sometimes we have to overcome other people's beliefs about us and prove them wrong)

Third Session—*A Chair for My Mother* (Literature)

1. Introduce the text and the following purposes for this read aloud:
   a. To map out the story elements

    b. To describe how characters feel and their point of view

2. Read the story aloud
3. After the read aloud, complete the story map anchor chart; discuss the author's use of a flashback to describe the fire
    a. Characters (girl, her mother, her grandma, cat)
    b. Setting (home, bank, store)
    c. Main problem/goal (the family's home burns; the rooms of their new apartment are very empty and they want a chair)
    d. Events (fire; afraid because Grandma was in the house; friends and neighbors gave them items for their apartment; they work to fill the jar)
    e. Resolution (they finally have the jar full; they go to bank to get bills for all the change; they go buy the chair)
4. After the read aloud, ask Raise the Bar questions:
    a. The author starts telling this story in the present tense. Let's look at the verbs in the story and notice what the author does throughout the story. What happens to the verbs? Why did the author do this? (author's craft)
    b. How did the little girl and her mother feel when they saw that their house was burning? (point of view, infer about characters' feelings)
    c. What were they most worried about when they saw the fire? (inferences) What in the text or illustrations helps you know that? (use text/illustrations to support thinking)
    d. After the fire, the community (neighbors and friends) brought them items to furnish their apartment. What was Grandma's response to that? (character's point of view)
    e. Why did Grandma say she "felt like Goldilocks in 'The Three Bears'" trying out all the chairs"? What is similar? (trying big, small, high, low, liking them or not liking them, finding one they liked best) What is different? (Goldilocks was in someone's house; there were only three chairs; she broke one of them) (compare/contrast across texts)
    f. Share about a time when you worked hard to earn something you wanted. How did it feel while you were waiting? After you got it? (experiential connection)
    g. What is the author's message? (central message) (we all face hardships; we have a choice in how we respond to hardships; if we work hard we can achieve what we want)

Fourth Session—*A Chair for My Mother* (Literature)

1. Introduce the text and the following purposes for this read aloud:
    a. To compare wants versus needs;

    b. To compare this story to the story *Amazing Grace*

2. Read the story aloud

3. After reading aloud, use a T-chart to compare wants versus needs
   a. What kinds of items would this family *need* immediately for their apartment after the fire?
   b. What items did the family *want* but would not need? (compare/contrast within text)

4. After the read aloud, review the story maps for *Amazing Grace* and *A Chair for My Mother*. Use them to compare the characters and problems in the two stories. Raise the Bar questions to ask during the discussion:
   a. How are the families in the two stories the same? (compare across texts)
   b. Tell me about the problem the main character faced in these two stories. How are the problems the same? (compare across texts) (both want something; both face hardship)
   c. How are the problems different? (contrast across texts) (hardship for Grace is caused by the attitudes/prejudices of her classmates; hardship in "Chair" is caused when the family loses everything they own in a house fire)
   d. Think of a time when you faced a problem. How did you handle it? (experiential connection)

Children's Book References

Ada, A. F., & Campoy, F. I. (2003). *¡Pío peep!: Traditional Spanish nursery rhymes*. New York, NY: Rayo.

Andersen, H. C., & Dusikova, M. (2012). *The princess and the pea*. Edinburgh, UK: Floris Books.

Asch, F. (1990). *Bear shadow*. New York, NY: Scholastic

Asch, F. (1993). *Moondance*. New York, NY: Scholastic.

Borges, L. J. (2009). *Seven nights*. New York, NY: New Directions.

Brett, J. (1996). *The mitten*. New York, NY: G. P. Putnam's Sons Books for Young Readers.

Brett, J. (1997). *The hat*. New York, NY: G. P. Putnam's Sons Books for Young Readers.

Brett, J. (2004). *The umbrella*. New York, NY: G. P. Putnam's Sons Books for Young Readers.

Bulla, C. R., & Otani, J. (1994). *What makes a shadow?* New York, NY: HarperCollins.

Carle, E. (1969). *The very hungry caterpillar*. New York, NY: Philomel Books.

Carle, E. (1989). *Animals, animals*. New York, NY: Philomel Books.

Cherry, L. (2000). *The great kapok tree: A tale of the Amazon rain forest*. Boston, MA: Houghton Mifflin.

Colandro, L., & Lee, J. D. (2014). *There was an old lady who swallowed a frog!* New York, NY: Cartwheel Books.

Cowley, J. (1999). *Mrs. Wishy Washy*. New York: NY: Philomel.

Crews, D. (1996). *Shortcut*. New York, NY: Greenwillow Books.

DePaola, T. (1975). *Strega Nona*. Englewood Cliffs, NJ: Prentice-Hall.

Drachman, E., & Muscarello, J. (2005). *A frog thing*. Los Angeles, CA: Kidwick Books.

Editors of *Time for Kids* & Satterfield, K. H. (2006). *Frogs! They are amazing amphibians*. New York, NY: HarperCollins.

Florian, D. (2001). *Lizards, frogs, and polliwogs*. San Diego, CA: Harcourt.

Florian, D. (2004). *Mammaliabilia*. New York, NY: Houghton Mifflin.

Forman, M. H. (1997). *From wax to crayon*. New York, NY: Children's Press.

Ghigna, C., & Speirs, J. (2004). *Animal tracks: Wild poems to read aloud*. New York, NY: Harry N. Abrams.

Gibbons, G. (1999). *Bats*. New York, NY: Holiday House.

Giovanni, N. (Ed.). (2008). *Hip hop speaks to children*. Naperville, IL: Sourcebooks Jabberwocky.

Greenburg, J. (2001). *Heart to heart: New poems inspired by twentieth-century American art*. New York, NY: Harry N. Abrams.

Heard, G., & Dewey, J. O. (1992). *Creatures of earth, sea, and sky*. Honesdale, PA: WordSong.

Henkes, K. (1993). *Owen*. New York, NY: Greenwillow Books.

Hoberman, M. A., & Emberley, M. (2012). *You read to me, I'll read to you: Very short fairy tales to read together.* New York, NY: Little, Brown Books for Young Readers.

Hoberman, M. A., & Fraser, B. (2006). *The llama who had no pajama: 100 favorite poems.* Boston, MA: Houghton Mifflin.

Hoffman, M., & Binch, C. (1991). *Amazing Grace.* New York, NY: Dial Books.

Hopkins, L. B., & Barbour, K. (2001). *Marvelous math: A book of poems.* New York, NY: Simon & Schuster Books for Young Readers.

Hurwitz, J., & Pinkney, J. (1993). *New shoes for Silvia.* New York, NY: HarperCollins.

Iorio, N. (2005). *Time for Kids: Bats!* New York, NY: HarperCollins.

Kalman, B., & Langille, J. (2005). *What are food chains and webs?* New York, NY: Crabtree.

Kroll, V., & Roundtree, K. (1995). *Jaha and Jamil went down the hill: An African Mother Goose.* Watertown, MA: Charlesbridge.

Lauber, P., & Keller, H. (1995). *Who eats what? Food chains and food webs.* New York, NY: HarperCollins.

Lear, E., & Brett, J. (1996). *The owl and the pussycat.* New York, NY: Puffin Books.

Lear, E., & Marshall, J. (1998). *The owl and the pussycat.* New York, NY: HarperCollins.

Lear, E., & Mortimer, A. (2006). *The owl and the pussycat.* New York, NY: Katherine Tegen Books.

Lewis, J. P. (2012). *National Geographic book of animal poetry: 200 poems with photographs that squeak, soar, and roar.* Washington, DC: National Geographic.

Lewis, J. P., & Desimini, L. (2002). *Doodle dandies: Poems that take shape.* New York, NY: Atheneum Books for Young Readers.

Littledale, F., & Pels, W. P. (1985). *The magic fish.* New York, NY: Scholastic.

Myer, A. (2012). *Delia's dull day: An incredibly boring story.* Ann Arbor, MI: Sleeping Bear Press.

Noble, T. H., & Kellogg, S. (1992). *The day Jimmy's boa ate the wash.* New York, NY: Puffin Books.

Parish, P., & Siebel, F. (1963). *Amelia Bedelia.* New York, NY: Greenwillow Books.

Pinkney, J. (2013). *The tortoise and the hare.* New York, NY: Little, Brown Books for Young Readers.

Piven, H. (2010). *My best friend is as sharp as a pencil: And other funny classroom portraits.* New York, NY: Schwartz & Wade.

Prelutsky, J., & Brown, M. (1986). *Read-aloud rhymes for the very young.* New York, NY: Knopf Book for Young Readers.

Prelutsky, J., Saint-Saens, C., & GrandPre, M. (2010). *The carnival of the animals.* New York, NY: Knopf Books for Young Readers

Rowden, J. (2005). *Paint me a poem: Poems inspired by masterpieces of art.* Honesdale, PA: WordSong.

Sendak, M. (1963). *Where the wild things are.* New York, NY: Harper & Row.

Van Allsburg, C. (1986). *The stranger.* Boston, MA: Houghton Mifflin.

Van Dusen, C. (2003). *A camping spree with Mr. McGee.* San Francisco, CA: Chronicle Books.

Viorst, J. (1987). *Alexander and the terrible, horrible, no good, very bad day.* New York, NY: Aladdin Paperbacks.

Wallace, K. (1998). *Tale of a tadpole.* New York, NY: DK.

Williams, V. B. (1982). *A chair for my mother.* New York, NY: Greenwillow Books.

Professional References

Barachetti, C., & Lavelli, M. (2011). Responsiveness of children with specific language impairment and maternal repairs during shared book reading. *International Journal of Language and Communication Disorders, 46*(5), 579–591. doi: 10.1111/j.1460-6984.2011.00032.x

Barone, D. M., & Xu, S. H. (2008). *Literacy instruction for English language learners, PreK–2.* New York, NY: Guilford.

Beck, I. L., & McKeown, M. (2001). Text talk: Capturing the benefits of read-aloud experiences for young children. *The Reading Teacher, 55*(1), 10–20.

Beck, I. L., & McKeown, M. (2007). Increasing young low-income children's oral vocabulary repertoires through rich and focused instruction. *The Elementary School Journal, 107*(3), 251–271. doi: 10.1086/511706

Beers, K. (2003). *When kids can't read, what teachers can do: A guide for teachers 6–12.* Portsmouth, NH: Heinemann.

Biemiller, A., & Boote, C. (2006). An effective method for building meaning vocabulary in primary grades. *Journal of Educational Psychology, 98*(1), 44–62. doi: 10.1037/0022-0663.98.1.44

Binger, C., Kent-Walsh, J., Berens, J., Del Campo, S., & Rivera, D. (2008). Teaching Latino parents to support the multi-symbol message productions of their children who require AAC. *Augmentative and Alternative Communication, 24*(4), 323–338. doi: 10.1080/07434610802130978

Birbili, M. (2006). Mapping knowledge: Concept maps in early childhood education. *Early Childhood Research and Practice, 8*(2). Retrieved from ecrp.uiuc.edu/v8n2/birbili.html

Bogard, J. M., & McMackin, M. C. (2012). Combining traditional and new literacies in a 21st-century writing workshop. *The Reading Teacher, 65*(5), 313–323. doi: 10.1002/trtr.01048

Bradley, B. A., & Price, L. H. (2011, December). *Engaging pre-kindergarten children in repeated readings of thematically related books.* Paper presented at the annual meeting of the Literacy Research Association, Jacksonville, FL.

Britsch, S. (2010). Photo-booklets for English language learning: Incorporating visual communication into early childhood teacher preparation. *Early Childhood Education Journal, 38*(3), 171–177. doi: 10.1007/s10643-010-0412-2

Browder, D. M., Mims, P. J., Spooner, F., Ahlgrim-Delzell, L., & Lee, A. (2008). Teaching elementary students with multiple disabilities to participate in shared stories. *Research and Practice for Persons with Severe Disabilities, 33*(1–2), 3–12.

Bruner, J. S. (1986). *Actual minds, possible worlds.* Cambridge, MA: Harvard University Press.

Christ, T., Wang, C., & Chiu, M. M. (2011). Using story dictation to support young children's vocabulary development: Outcomes and process. *Early Childhood Research Quarterly, 26*, 30–41. doi: 10.1016/j.ecresq.2010.06.002

Collins, M. (2010). ELL preschoolers' English vocabulary acquisition from storybook reading. *Early Childhood Research Quarterly, 25*(1), 84–97. doi: 10.1016/j.ecresq.2009.07.009

de Jong, M. T., & Bus, A. G. (2002). Quality of book-reading matters for emergent readers: An experiment with the same book in a regular or electronic format. *Journal of Educational Psychology, 94*(1), 145–155. doi: 10.1037/0022-0663.94.1.145

Dickinson, D. K., & Smith, M. W. (1991). Preschool talk: Patterns of teacher-child interaction in early childhood classrooms. *Journal of Research in Childhood Education, 6*(1), 20–29. doi: 10.1080/02568549109594819

Dodd, J. L. (2012). Adapted stories: Creating accessible stories for children with complex language problems. *Perspectives on Language Learning and Education, 19*, 139–146. doi: 10.1044/lle19.4.139

Dodici, B. J., Draper, D. C., & Peterson, C. A. (2003). Early parent-child interactions and early literacy development. *Topics in Early Childhood Special Education, 23*(3), 124–136. doi: 10.1177/02711214030230030301

Donovan, C. A., Milewicz, E. J., & Smolkin, L. B. (2003). Beyond the single text: Nurturing young children's interest in reading and writing for multiple purposes. *Young Children, 58*(2), 30–36.

Duke, N. K. (2000). 3.6 minutes per day: The scarcity of informational texts in first grade. *Reading Research Quarterly, 35*(2), 202–224.

Duke, N. K., & Kays, J. (1998). "Can I say 'Once upon a time'?": Kindergarten children developing knowledge of information book language. *Early Childhood Research Quarterly, 13*(2), 295–318. doi: 10.1016/S0885-2006(99)80041-6

Elster, C. A., & Hanauer, D. I. (2002). Voicing texts, voices around texts: "Reading poems in elementary school classrooms." *Research in the Teaching of English, 37*(1), 89–134.

Facella, M. A., Rampino, K. M., & Shea, E. K. (2005). Effective teaching strategies for English language learners. *Bilingual Research Journal, 29*(1), 209–221. doi: 10.1080/15235882.2005.10162832

Fisher, D., & Frey, N. (2012). Close reading in elementary schools. *The Reading Teacher, 66*(3), 179–188. doi: 10.1002/TRTR.01117

Gambrell, L. B., & Jawitz, P. B. (1993). Mental imagery, text illustrations, and children's story comprehension and recall. *Reading Research Quarterly, 28*, 265–273. doi: 10.2307/747998

Gerde, H. K., & Powell, D. R. (2009). Teacher education, book-reading practices, and children's language growth across one year of Head Start. *Early Education and Development, 20*(2), 211–237. doi: 10.1080/10409280802595417

Gibbons, P. (2003). Mediating language learning: Teacher interactions with ESL students in a content-based classroom. *TESOL Quarterly, 37*(2), 247–273. doi: 10.2307/3588504

Gillanders, C., & Castro, D. C. (2011). Storybook reading for young dual language learners. *Young Children, 66*(1), 91–95.

Halpren, R. (2013). Tying early childhood education more closely to schooling: Promise, perils, and practical problems. *Teachers College Record, 115*, 1–28.

Hammett, L. A., van Kleeck, A., & Huberty, C. J. (2003). Patterns of parents' extratextual interactions during book sharing with preschool children: A cluster analysis study. *Reading Research Quarterly, 38*(4), 442–467. doi: 10.1598/RRQ.38.4.2

Hargrave, A. C., & Sénéchal, M. (2000). A book reading intervention with preschool children who have limited vocabularies: The benefits of regular reading and dialogic reading. *Early Childhood Research Quarterly, 15*(1), 75–90. doi: 10.1016/S0885-2006(99)00038-1

Harste, J. C., Woodward, V. A., & Burke, C. L. (1984). *Language stories and literacy lessons*. Portsmouth, NH: Heinemann.

Harvey, S., & Goudvis, A. (2007). *Strategies that work* (2nd ed.). Portland, ME: Stenhouse.

Heard, G. (2012). *Poetry lessons to meet the Common Core State Standards: Exemplar poems with engaging lessons and response activities that help students read, understand, and appreciate poetry*. New York, NY: Scholastic Teaching Resources.

Heflin, B. R., & Barksdale-Ladd, M. A. (2001). African American children's literature that helps students find themselves: Selection guidelines for grades K–3. *The Reading Teacher, 54*(8), 810–819.

Higgins, J. J. (n.d.). School of Education at Johns Hopkins University–Multicultural children's literature: Creating and applying an evaluation tool in response to the needs of urban educators. *New Horizons for Learning*. Retrieved from education.jhu.edu/PD/newhorizons/strategies/topics/multicultural-education/multicultural-childrens-literature/

Hoffman, J. L., & Paciga, K. A. (2014). Click, swipe, and read: Sharing e-books with toddlers and preschoolers. *Early Childhood Education Journal, 42*, 379–388. doi: 10.1007/s10643-013-0622-5

Kaderavek, J. N., & Justice, L. (2002). Shared storybook reading as an intervention context: Practices and potential pitfalls. *American Journal of Speech-Language Pathology, 11*, 395–406. doi: 10.1044/1058-0360(2002/043)

Kaderavek, J. N., & Justice, L. M. (2005). The effect of book genre in the repeated readings of mothers and their children with language impairment: A pilot investigation. *Child Language Teaching and Therapy, 21*, 75–92. doi: 10.1191/0265659005ct282oa

Kim, J. E., & Anderson, J. (2008). Mother-child shared reading with print and digital texts. *Journal of Early Childhood Literacy, 8*(2), 213–245. doi: 10.1177/1468798408091855

Klesius, J. P., & Griffith, P. L. (1996). Interactive storybook reading for at-risk learners. *The Reading Teacher, 49*, 552–560.

Kontos, S., & Wilcox-Herzog, A. (1997). Teachers' interactions with children: Why are they so important? *Young Children, 52*(2), 4–12.

Korat, O., Shamir, A., & Arbiv, L. (2011). E-books as support for emergent writing with and without adult assistance. *Educational and Information Technology, 16*, 301–318. doi: 10.1007/s10639-010-9127-7

Koskinen, P. S., Blum, I. H., Bisson, S. A., Phillips, S. M., Creamer, T. S., & Baker, T. K. (2000). Book access, shared reading, and audio models: The effects of supporting the literacy learning of linguistically diverse students in school and at home. *Journal of Educational Psychology, 92*(1), 23–36. doi: 10.1037/0022-0663.92.1.23

Labbo, L. D., Eakle, J. A., & Montero, K. M. (2002, May). Digital language experience approach: Using digital photographs and software as a language experience approach innovation. *Reading Online*, 24–43. Retrieved from www.readingonline.org/electronic/elec_index.asp?HREF=labbo2/index.html

Labbo, L. D., & Norguerón-Liu, S. (2014). Digital reading and writing: Pedagogy for the digital child. In D. R. Reutzel (Ed.), *Handbook of research-based practices in early education* (pp. 175–192). New York, NY: Guilford Press.

Lanter, E., & Watson, L. R. (2008). Promoting literacy in students with ASD: The basics for the SLP. *Language, Speech, and Hearing Services in Schools, 39*(1), 33–43. doi: 10.1044/0161-1461(2008/004)

Larson, L. C. (2010). Digital readers: The next chapter in e-book reading and response. *The Reading Teacher, 64*(1), 15–22. doi: 10.1598/RT.64.1.2

Lefever-Davis, S., & Pearman, C. (2005). Early readers and electronic texts: CD-ROM storybook features that influence reading behaviors. *The Reading Teacher, 58*(5), 446–454. doi: 10.1598/RT.58.5.4

Lim, Y. S., & Cole, K. N. (2002). Facilitating first language development in young Korean children through parent training in picture book interactions. *Bilingual Research Journal, 26*(2), 367–381. doi: 10.1080/15235882.2002.10668716

Lipson, M. Y., Valencia, S. W., Wixson, K. K., & Peters, C. W. (1993). Integration and thematic teaching: Integration to improve teaching and learning. *Language Arts, 70*(4), 252–263.

Louie, B. Y. (2006). Guiding principles for teaching multicultural literature. *The Reading Teacher, 59*(5), 438–448. doi: 10.1598/RT.59.5.3

Lynch, J. S., & van den Broek, P. (2007). Understanding the glue of narrative structure: Children's on- and off-line inferences about characters' goals. *Cognitive Development, 22*, 323–340. doi: 10.1016/j.cogdev.2007.02.002

Maloch, B. (2008). Beyond exposure: The uses of informational texts in a second grade classroom. *Research in the Teaching of English, 42*(2), 315–362.

Martinez, M., & Teale, W. (1993). Teacher storybook reading style: A comparison of six teachers. *Research in the Teaching of English, 27*, 175–199.

Marzano, R. J., Pickering, D. J., & Pollock, J. E. (2001). *Classroom instruction that works: Research-based strategies for increasing student achievement.* Alexandria, VA: Association for Supervision and Curriculum Development.

McCollin, M., & O'Shea, D. (2005). Increasing reading achievement of students from culturally and linguistically diverse backgrounds. *Preventing School Failure, 50*(1), 41–44. doi: 10.3200/PSFL.50.1.41-44

McGee, L. M., & Schickedanz, J. A. (2007). Repeated interactive read-alouds in preschool and kindergarten. *The Reading Teacher, 60*(8), 742–751. doi: 10.1598/RT.60.8.4

McGinty, A. S., Justice, L. M., Zucker, T. A., Gosse, C, & Skibbe, L. E. (2012). Shared-reading dynamics: Mothers' question use and the verbal participation of children with specific language impairment. *Journal of Speech, Language, and Hearing Research, 55*, 1039–1052. doi: 10.1044/1092-4388(2011/10-0298)

McGinty, A., Sofka, A., Sutton, M., & Justice, L. (2006). Fostering print awareness through interactive shared reading. In van Kleeck (Ed.), *Sharing books and stories to promote language and literacy* (pp. 77–120). San Diego, CA: Plural.

Meller, W. B., Richardson, D., & Hatch, J. A. (2009). Using read-alouds with critical literacy literature in K–3 classrooms. *Young Children, 64*(6), 76–78.

Meyer, A., Rose, D. H., & Gordon, D. (2013). *Universal design for learning: Theory and practice.* Wakefield, MA: CAST.

Meyer, L. A., Stahl, S. A., Wardrop, J. L., & Linn, R. L. (1994). Effects of reading storybooks aloud to children. *Journal of Educational Research, 88*(2), 69–85. doi: 10.1080/00220671.1994.9944821

Moline, S. (2011). *I see what you mean: Visual literacy K–8* (2nd ed.). Portland, ME: Stenhouse.

Moody, A. K., Justice, L. M., & Cabell, S. Q. (2010). Electronic versus traditional storybooks: Relative influence on preschool children's engagement and communication. *Journal of Early Childhood Literacy, 10*(3), 294–313. doi: 10.1177/1468798410372162

Morgan, H. (2013). Multimodal children's e-books help young learners in reading. *Early Childhood Education Journal, 41*, 477–483. doi: 10.1007/s10643-013-0575-8

Morrow, L. M. (2003). Motivating lifelong voluntary readers. In J. Flood, D. Lapp, J. Squire, & J. Jensen (Eds.), *Handbook of research on teaching the English language arts* (2nd ed., pp. 857–867). Mahwah, NJ: Erlbaum.

Morrow, L. M., & Gambrell, L. B. (2002). Literature-based instruction in the early years. In S. B. Neuman & D. K. Dickinson (Eds.), *Handbook of early literacy research* (pp. 348–360). New York, NY: Guilford.

National Association for the Education of Young Children. (2011). *The Common Core State Standards: Caution and opportunity for early childhood education.* Washington, DC: Authors.

National Governors Association Center for Best Practices & Council of Chief State School Officers. (2010). *Common Core State Standards for English language arts and literacy in history/social studies, science, and technical subjects.* Washington, DC: Authors.

Neuman, S. B., & Dwyer, J. (2011). Developing vocabulary and conceptual knowledge for low-income preschoolers: A design experiment. *Journal of Literacy Research, 43*(2), 103–129. doi: 10.1177/1086296X11403089

Neuman, S. B., & Gallagher, P. (1994). Joining together in literacy learning: Teenage mothers and children. *Reading Research Quarterly, 29*, 383–401. doi: 10.2307/747786

Neuman, S. B., Newman, E. H., & Dwyer, J. (2011). Educational effects of a vocabulary intervention on preschoolers' word knowledge and conceptual development: A cluster-randomized trial. *Reading Research Quarterly, 46*(3), 249–272. doi: 10.1598/RRQ46.3.3

Neuman, S. B., Pinkham, A., & Kaefer, T. (2015). Supporting vocabulary teaching and learning in prekindergarten: The role of educative curriculum materials. *Early Education and Development.* doi: 10.1080/ 10409289.2015.1004517

Neuman, S. B., & Wright, T. S. (2013). *All about words: Increasing vocabulary in the Common Core classroom, PreK–2.* New York, NY: Teachers College Press.

No Child Left Behind Act of 2001. Pub. L. No. 107-110, § 115, Stat. 1425 (2002).

Pearson, P. D., & Gallagher, M. C. (1983). The instruction of reading comprehension. *Contemporary Educational Psychology, 8*(3), 317–344.

Pentimonti, J. M., & Justice, L. M. (2010). Teachers' use of scaffolding strategies during read alouds in the preschool classroom. *Early Childhood Education Journal, 37*, 241–248. doi: 10.1007/s10643-009-0348-6

Price, L. H., & Bradley, B. (2009, December). *A qualitative analysis of preschool teachers' talk during book sharing with storybooks and with expository books.* Paper presented at the annual meeting of the National Reading Conference, Albuquerque, NM.

Price, L. H., & Bradley, B. (2011, December). *Pre-kindergarten teachers' preferences when choosing information books.* Paper presented at the annual conference of the Literacy Research Association, Jacksonville, FL.

Price, L. H., Bradley, B. A., & Smith, J. M. (2012). A comparison of preschool teachers' talk during storybook and information book read-alouds. *Early Childhood Research Quarterly, 27*, 426–440. doi: 10.1016/j.ecresq.2012.02.003

Price, L. H., & Ruscher, K. Y. (2006). Fostering phonological awareness using shared book reading and an embedded explicit approach. In van Kleeck (Ed.), *Sharing books and stories to promote language and literacy* (pp. 15–76). San Diego, CA: Plural.

Proctor-Williams, K., Fey, M., & Frome Loeb, D. (2001). Parental recasts and production of copulas and articles by children with specific language impairment and typical language. *American Journal of Speech Language Pathology, 10*, 155–168. doi: 10.1044/1058-0360(2001/015)

Pullen, P. C., & Justice, L. M. (2003). Enhancing phonological awareness, print awareness, and oral language skills in preschool children. *Intervention in School and Clinic, 39*(2), 87–98. doi: 10.1177/10534512030390020401

Rabidoux, P. C., & MacDonald, J. D. (2000). An interactive taxonomy of mothers and children during storybook interactions. *American Journal of Speech-Language Pathology, 9*(4), 331–344. doi: 10.1044/1058-0360.0904.331

Restrepo, M. A., Morgan, G. P., & Thompson, M. S. (2013). The efficacy of a vocabulary intervention for dual-language learners with language impairment. *Journal of Speech, Language, and Hearing Research, 56*(2), 748–765. doi: 10.1044/1092-4388(2012/11-0173)

Schugar, H. T., Smith, C. A., & Schugar, J. T. (2013). Teaching with interactive picture e-books in grades K–6. *The Reading Teacher, 66*(8), 615–624. doi: 10.1002/trtr.1168

Schwarz, A. L., van Kleeck, A., Beaton, D., Horne, E., MacKenzie, H., & Abdi, H. (2015). A read-aloud storybook selection system for pre-readers at the preschool language level: A pilot study. *Journal of Speech, Language, and Hearing Research, 58*(4), 1273–1291. doi: 10.1044/2015_JSLHR-L-15-0056

Serafini, F. (2013). Close readings and children's literature. *The Reading Teacher, 67*(4), 299–301. doi: 10.1002/trtr.1213

Shamir, A., & Korat, O. (2009). The educational electronic book as a tool for supporting children's emergent literacy. In A. Bus & S. B. Neuman (Eds.), *Multimedia and literacy development* (pp. 168–181). New York, NY: Routledge.

Shamir, A., Korat, O., & Fellah, R. (2012). Promoting vocabulary, phonological awareness, and concept about print among children at risk for learning disability: Can e-books help? *Reading and Writing, 25*, 45–69. doi: 10.1007/s11145-010-9247-x

Singleton, N. C., & Saks, J. (2015). Co-speech gesture input as a support for language learning in children with and without early language delay. *Perspectives on Language Learning and Education, 22*(2), 61–71.

Skibbe, L. E., Moody, A. J., Justice, L. M, & McGinty, A. S. (2010). Socio-emotional climate of storybook reading interactions for mothers and preschoolers with language impairment. *Reading and Writing, 23*, 53–71. doi: 10.1007/s11145-008-9149-3

Smolkin, L. B., & Donovan, C. A. (2001). The contexts of comprehension: The information book read aloud, comprehension acquisition, and comprehension instruction in a first grade classroom. *Elementary School Journal, 102*(2), 97–122. doi: 10.1086/499695

Stahl, S. A. (2003). What do we expect storybook reading to do? How storybook reading impacts word recognition. In A. Van Kleeck, S. A. Stahl, & E. B. Bauer (Eds.), *On reading books to children: Parents and teachers* (pp. 363–383). Mahwah, NJ: Lawrence Erlbaum.

Taylor, B. M., Pearson, P. D., Clark, K. F., & Walpole, S. (1999). *Beating the odds in teaching all children to read* (CIERA Report #2-006). Ann Arbor, MI: Center for the Improvement of Early Reading Achievement.

Taylor, B. M., Pearson, P. D., Peterson, D., & Rodriquez, M. C. (2002). *The CIERA school change project: Supporting schools as they implement home-grown reading reform.* Ann Arbor, MI: Center for the Improvement of Early Reading Achievement.

Trudeau, N., Cleave, P. L., & Woelk, E. J. (2003). Using augmentative and alternative communication approaches to promote participation of preschoolers during book reading: A pilot study. *Child Language Teaching and Therapy, 19*(2), 181–210. doi: 10.1191=0265659003ct250oa

Ukrainetz, T. A. (1998). Stickwriting stories: A quick and easy narrative representation strategy. *Language, Speech, and Hearing Services in Schools, 29*, 197–206. doi: 10.1044/0161-1461.2904.197

van den Broek, P. (2001). *The role of television viewing in the development of reading comprehension.* Ann Arbor, MI: Center for the Improvement of Early Reading Achievement.

van Kleeck, A. (2008). Providing preschool foundations for later reading comprehension: The importance of and ideas for targeting inferences in storybook-sharing interventions. *Psychology in the Schools, 45*(7), 627–643. doi: 10.1002/pits.20314

van Kleeck, A. (2014). Distinguishing between casual talk and academic talk beginning in the preschool years: An important consideration for speech-language pathologists. *American Journal of Speech Language Pathology, 23*, 724–741. doi: 10.1044/2014_AJSLP-14-0032

van Kleeck, A. (2003). Research on book sharing: Another critical look. In A. van Kleeck, S. A. Stahl, & E. B. Bauer (Eds.), *On reading books to children: Parents and teachers* (pp. 271–320). Mahwah, NJ: Lawrence Erlbaum.

van Kleeck, A., Stahl, S. A., & Bauer, E. B. (Eds.). (2003). *On reading books to children: Parents and teachers.* Mahwah, NJ: Lawrence Erlbaum.

Vogler-Elias, D. (2009). *A parent-implemented shared storybook reading intervention for preschoolers with autism spectrum disorders.* Buffalo, NY: State University of New York at Buffalo.

Vygotsky, L. S. (1962). *Thought and language.* Cambridge, MA: MIT Press.

Wasik, B. A., Bond, M. A., & Hindman, A. (2006). The effects of a language and literacy intervention on Head Start children and teachers. *Journal of Educational Psychology, 98*(1), 63–74. doi: 10.1037/0022-0663.98.1.63

Welsch, J. G. (2008). Playing within and beyond the story: Encouraging book-related pretend play. *The Reading Teacher, 62*(2), 138–148. doi: 10.1598/RT.62.2.5

Wilhelm, J. (2013). *Action strategies for deepening comprehension: Role plays, text-structure tableaux, talking statues, and others.* New York, NY: Scholastic Teaching Resources.

Yokota, J., & Teale, W. H. (2014). Picture books and the digital world: Educators making informed choices. *The Reading Teacher, 67*(8), 577–585. doi: 10.1002/trtr.1262

Yopp, R. H., & Yopp, H. K. (2006). Informational texts as read-alouds at school and home. *Journal of Literacy Research, 38*(1), 37–51. doi: 10.1207/s15548430jlr3801_2

Zipprich, M., Grace, M., & Grote-Garcia, S. A. (2009). Building story schema: Using patterned books as a means of instruction for students with disabilities. *Intervention in School and Clinic, 44*(5), 294–299. doi: 10.1177/1053451208330896

Index

About the Authors

Lisa Hammett Price, PhD, CCC-SLP, is a professor in the speech-language pathology program in the Department of Communication Disorders, Special Education, and Disability Services at Indiana University of Pennsylvania (IUP). In 2011, she and her colleagues Anne van Kleeck and Carl J. Huberty received the Dina Feitelson Research Award from the International Reading Association for their 2009 journal article published in *Reading Research Quarterly*. Price specializes in pediatric speech-language disorders, with an emphasis on language and literacy assessment and intervention for children with language disorders. She has 15 years of experience working as a clinical speech-language pathologist with families and their children 2 to 12 years old. She uses book reading and thematic units as methods for targeting language weaknesses while increasing students' access to the curriculum. Her research has focused on parent-child and teacher-child interactions during book reading, looking for how adult scaffolding can better support child language growth. She also uses different genres of books to achieve different learning objectives. Price received her PhD in communication sciences and disorders with a specialization in child language and literacy from the University of Georgia and her bachelor's and master's degrees in the same field from James Madison University in Virginia.

Barbara A. Bradley, PhD, is an associate professor in the Department of Curriculum and Teaching at the University of Kansas (KU). She is a former preschool teacher, working with students with special needs for 14 years. She has spent the past 10 years teaching preservice and inservice teachers at the university level to prepare them to teach reading across the lifespan. Bradley specializes in early literacy and design research methods. She has conducted research funded by both external and internal grants on early literacy and beginning reading, the use of design research to investigate instructional coaching, and the use of technology to support instructional practices and student learning. She has published extensively on these topics and is well respected in the field. Bradley received her PhD from the University of Georgia in reading education, her master's degree from Adelphi University in physical education, and her two bachelor's degrees from the State University of New York at Stony Brook in biology and psychology.

Printed and bound by CPI Group (UK) Ltd, Croydon, CR0 4YY

09/06/2025

14685981-0004